TRAILS WEST

TEACH ME
TO DO IT
MYSELF

Montessori activities for you and your child

Maja Pitamic

BARRON'S

OCT. 06

First edition for the United States, and its dependencies published in 2004 by Barron's Educational Series, Inc.

All inquiries should be addressed to:
Barron's Educational Series, Inc.
250 Wireless Boulevard
Hauppauge, New York 11788
http://www.barronseduc.com

Library of Congress Catalog Card No.: 2003111621
International Standard Book No.: 0-7641-2789-6

Conceived and produced by Elwin Street Limited
35 Charlotte Road
London EC2A 3PD
www.elwinstreet.com

Designer and Illustrator: Isabel Alberdi
Photography: Keith Waterton

Printed and bound in China
987654321

The activities described in this book are to be carried out with parental supervision at all times. Every effort has been made by to ensure the safety of activities detailed. Neither the author nor the publishers shall be liable or responsible for any harm or damage done allegedly arising from any information or suggestion in this book. *Teach Me to Do it Myself* has been written by a qualified Montessori teacher but is not approved, endorsed or affiliated with Montessori in any way.

The publishers would like to thank the following for their participation in this book:
Elizabeth and Lily Nugent; Francesca and Steven de Munnich Langford; Carole and Ben Markey; Anouk, Jeremy, and Audrey Assouly; Ronnie Planalp and Jackson Trevor; Kalpana and Rohan Prabhakar; Susie and Phoebe Dart

Contents

Preface

This is a fun-filled practical activity book for children between the ages of three and five. The activities are based on the Montessori teaching philosophy and will give your child the best possible start in achieving essential skills and developing a greater understanding of the world around him.

You act as a guide, taking your child through the activities, to build an essential repertoire of life skills that range from dressing to basic science. No specialized knowledge is required.

The activities go step by step, and include suggestions for future activities. Only simple preparation is required, with materials that are available in most homes.

Not only will your child develop his coordination and grow in confidence and self-esteem, you will gain greater insight into your child's development. Best of all, you will be teaching your child to do things for himself, and setting him on the road to independence.

Who was Montessori?

Born in Rome in 1870, Maria Montessori became the first female medical graduate of Rome University. She was the director of the Scuola Ortofrenica, a school for children with special education needs, and by 1900 she was teaching Pedagogical Anthropology at Rome University.

In 1907 Montessori opened the first Case dei Bambini, a school for children from the slums. While there, she devised her now world-famous teaching method. Word spread quickly of the revolutionary teaching method that was being employed in the school, and soon visitors were flocking to observe. The Montessori teaching method became internationally renowned.

Possibly Montessori's most revolutionary belief was the importance of the child's environment when learning. She felt that for children to flourish and grow in self-esteem, they needed to work in a child-centered environment. Today, not only Montessori schools, but all schools recognize the part that the environment has to play in the development of the child.

Montessori always claimed that she did not devise a teaching method but that her ideas on teaching children merely grew out of close observation of children. From this, she discovered the following needs:

- Joy in learning
- Love of order
- The need to be independent
- The need to be respected and listened to
- Interest in fact and fiction

Montessori maintained these needs were universal, regardless of nationality, gender, race, or background of a child. Today, more than 50

years since Montessori's death in 1952, these needs remain unchanged and are as relevant now as when they were first observed in 1909.

This book presents my interpretation of Montessori drawn from my years of teaching. The activities follow the "spirit," rather than the letter, of Montessori.

How to use this book

This book is based on key Montessori principles of learning through experience, but rest assured there is no need to create a Montessori classroom in your own home. The activities require little preparation and use readily available materials. You may be worried that you do not have a specialized knowledge of teaching, but do not worry! The points set out below will guide you through the essential steps when presenting an activity for your child:

■ To avoid repetition, the use of "she" and "he" is alternated. All the activities are suitable for boys and girls.

■ Check your environment. Make sure that you and your child can do the activity in comfort and safety.

■ Make sure that your child can see the activity clearly. Sit your child to the left of you (to your right, if she is left-handed).

■ Aim to work with your right hand (your left hand, if your child is left-handed) for consistency.

■ Many of the activities are done on a tray. This defines the work space for your child. Choose a tray that is not patterned, to avoid distraction.

■ Prepare the activity in advance. There is no point suggesting an activity to a child only to discover that you don't have the materials.

Tip box ■ If you don't know the answer to a question, say that you don't know, and see if you can find out the answer together.

■ Although a structured approach is needed, be prepared to be flexible and don't worry if things don't always go as planned; it may lead your child down unexpected paths of discovery and that's when things get exciting.

■ Be orderly when presenting the activity. Set out your materials in an orderly way and this will instill in your child a sense of order.

■ Make your child responsible for taking the materials to the work space and then returning them when the activity is completed. This creates a "cycle of work," and encourages your child to focus on the project.

■ Be clear in your own mind what the aim of the activity is, so always read the exercise through first.

■ Do not interrupt when your child is working. Learn to sit back and observe.

■ Try not to be negative. If your child is unable to do the activity correctly, then make a mental note to reintroduce it again at a later stage.

■ If your child is absorbed by the activity and wishes to

repeat it, let her do so as many times as she wishes. A child learns through repetition.

■ Create a work area for your child, if space permits. When an activity is over, leave the activity in a safe place so that your child can return to it if she wishes.

■ If your child abuses any of the materials in the activity, then the activity needs to be removed immediately. By doing this, she will understand that her behavior was unacceptable. The activity can be reintroduced at a later date.

Frequently asked questions

How old should my child be before she is presented with an activity?

■ I have deliberately not set ages for the activities, as this can cause panic in parents if their child does not want to do a particular activity. Each child is an individual with different strengths and weaknesses, and it is very rare to find a child who is confident in all areas of study. As a guideline, in a Montessori classroom, children are generally introduced to the activities in Chapters One and Two first, as these make a good foundation for the rest of the activities.

For children between the ages of four and five, I would suggest that you introduce a selection of activities from all the chapters. The exception to this is if you see that your child has a particular interest in a subject, for example, mathematics, then present more of the numeracy activities.

Do I need to follow the order of the activities?

■ Aim to take each chapter in the order given, as they follow a natural progression. There is some flexibility in Chapters One, Two, and Five; you can try an activity, and return to it at a later stage, if necessary. If your child already knows the alphabet, or the numerals up to ten, you might be able to introduce a later activity. However, it does not hurt to review knowledge, and it can increase a child's confidence.

If an activity is graded, when can my child progress to the next level of the activity?

■ In the sections called "Other activities to try," you will find progression activities that are ordered from easiest to hardest. Once your child has mastered one activity and she feels confident to work independently, then present the next level of the activity.

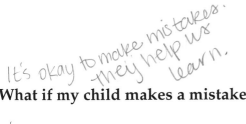

It's okay to make mistakes. they help us learn.

What if my child makes a mistake?

■ Encourage your child to work with care and attention, and remember that you also need to do so. Try not to point out your child's mistake, but find a way for her to correct her own mistakes. In this way, she will come to regard mistakes as something to learn from. Too often I have worked with children who are unwilling to try new activities for fear of making a mistake.

When is the best time in the day to present the activities?

■ Children, like adults, have times during the day when they are more receptive. The majority of children are at their most receptive during the morning, so any language and numeracy activities should definitely be done during this time. The other activities can be done at any time, but I would advise against going beyond mid-afternoon.

What if my child does not seem to respond to the activity?

■ If your child seems to be showing no interest in the activity, do not worry or get cross with your child. Simply put the activity away. Go through with yourself the presentation points. Ask yourself, did I present the activity in an appealing way? Was it the right time of the day? Did I understand my aim and did my child understand what was required? If it was a language or numeracy activity, consider whether your child was ready for this activity.

How do we use the worksheets?

■ When using the worksheets at the back of the book, copy them onto 11 x 17-inch (28 x 35-cm; A3) paper first, enlarging them to fit the full paper size. This way there should be plenty of space for your child to use each worksheet and they can be used many times over.

Life skills

The activities in this chapter will equip your child with important life skills.

To an adult these tasks may appear very simple because once mastered they are carried out automatically. But your child will experience a sense of accomplishment and self-worth when she is able to carry out these activities independently.

The first group of activities teach basic personal hygiene, such as washing hands and brushing hair. Further activities include putting on shoes and learning to pour, which have the benefit of helping your child develop hand–eye coordination.

Washing hands

What could be more fundamental than washing and drying your hands, and yet many children start school without this skill. Imagine how proud and confident your child will feel if she knows how to wash her hands when asked to do so. Using a sink can be quite tricky for a child at first; start with a bowl of water, as explained here.

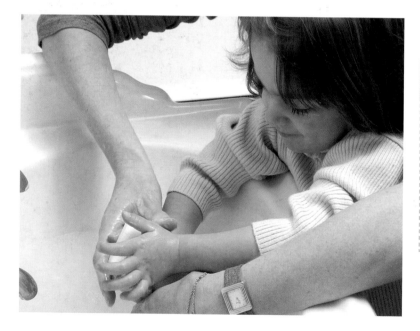

You will need

- Large plastic bowl
- Tray
- Bar of soap on a soap dish or pump soap dispenser
- Medium pitcher, filled with warm water
- 2 hand towels

When to wash hands

When your child has mastered washing her hands, explain why and when we need to wash our hands. After using the toilet, before meals, and before cooking, remind your child to wash her hands, until she remembers for herself. Remember to lead by example!

1. Place the bowl on the tray with the other items to the right (or left, if your child is left handed). Half-fill the bowl with water.

2. Wet your hands and rub soap over your hands slowly so that your child can see that you are covering your hands with the soap. Replace the soap back on the dish, or, if you are using a pump dispenser, remind your child that you need only one or two squirts.

3. Rinse your hands in the water. Dry your hands using a towel, again slowly, so your child can see you drying all parts of your hands.

4. As you replace the dirty water with clean water, ask her why the water needs to be changed before she washes her hands. (Show her the dirty water as a clue.) Invite your child to try.

Other activities to try

Show your child how to wash her hands at a sink. With your child standing on a stool, show how to: use the plug; turn on the faucets (a quarter turn), and turn off again; check the temperature of the water; release the plug when finished.

Show your child how to cover her mouth when coughing, and explain why this is important.

Cleaning teeth

If ever there was a good habit that should be learned at an early age, then cleaning your teeth is it. Enlist the support of your dentist, who will help to explain why and when we need to clean our teeth. Take this opportunity to explain why we need to brush our teeth, and when, including after meals, bedtime, and why we don't share toothbrushes and towels.

1 Put out the materials, with the mirror in the center. Half-fill one cup with water and put it to the right of the bowl. Keep your child's toothbrush, cup, and towel on the tray, and place out of reach until it is his turn.

2 Release the top of the toothpaste tube and squeeze out a small amount (no bigger than the size of a pea).

3 Brush your teeth and gums slowly, while looking in the mirror. This will help your child to understand how to use the mirror.

4 Rinse out your mouth with water from the cup. With the remaining water, pour over the toothbrush and clean the bristles. Wipe your mouth with a towel.

5 Bring out your child's materials, and make sure they are set out in the same positions you had before.

You will need

- 2 toothbrushes
- Large plastic bowl
- 2 cups
- Tube of toothpaste
- Face mirror on a stand
- Medium pitcher, filled with water
- 2 hand towels
- Tray

Other activities to try

When your child needs to brush his teeth again, take him to the sink and repeat the task there. Have a footstool and mirror in place so he can reach and see clearly.

Brushing hair

Both boys and girls are fascinated by the task of brushing hair. I have watched children absorbed in this activity through satisfaction of a skill mastered and a pride in their appearance.

You will need

- Face mirror on a stand
- 2 hairbrushes (one for you, one for your child)

Other activities to try

Introduce a wide-toothed comb and show how it can be used to remove knots gently.

Show your child how to wash her brush and comb, and explain why.

Show how to make a ponytail using a doll.

Teach your child how to braid long hair using a doll.

1 Place the mirror in the center of the table. Put your brush in front of the mirror, and your child's brush out of the way.

2 Brush your hair with slow, gentle strokes, turning your head so that you brush both sides. Use the mirror, and explain what you are doing.

3 Move the mirror so your child can see, and set the brush in front of the mirror, for your child to try.

Folding clothes

This activity begins very simply with folding handkerchiefs, and then moves on to folding clothes. When selecting clothes for your child to fold, choose clothes that have seams that can act as a guideline, for example, a shirt or sweater. Take the opportunity to explain why we need to fold clothes, and once folded, where clothes need to be kept. You could even stick pictures of clothing on different drawers as a reminder.

1 Mark an old handkerchief using the pen and ruler, with a vertical and horizontal line. Put the handkerchief and clothes to be folded in the basket.

2 Take the handkerchief from the basket and place it flat on the table. Fold it along the marker lines. Open the handkerchief, and pass it to your child to try.

3 Repeat the exercise, but use a handkerchief with no marker guidelines.

4 Move onto folding the clothes. Take one item of clothing at a time. Fold in the way of your choice, but aim to be consistent so your child can copy. If you fold over a right sleeve first, always start this way, whether folding a shirt or sweater.

You will need

- Old handkerchiefs
- Red felt pen
- A ruler
- A selection of your child's clothes
- Large basket to put the clothes in

Putting on a coat

Here is a quick and fun way for your child to put on his coat by himself.

Other activities to try

Take your family's washed socks (not more than four pairs to begin with), and place on a table. Find one of each pair and lay out in a row. Now ask your child to find each matching sock, and to place one on top of the other to make a pair. When all the socks are matched, show your child how to roll them up, and fold over to make into a ball.

Put folded clothes away in drawers and closets. Practice this with your child each time you do some laundry.

Using a favorite sweater, practice turning the sleeves right-side out. Move on to whole items of clothing.

1 Put the coat on the floor, inside facing up, and ask your child to stand facing the neck end of the coat.

2 Ask him to squat down and put his arms into the sleeves.

3 As he stands up, ask him to swing his arms up and around, to finish with his arms by his sides and the coat on.

Buttoning a shirt

This is a complex activity that has been broken down into easy stages so your child can understand each stage. One of the main difficulties children have with this skill is ensuring that the ends of the shirt are lined up so that they don't run out of buttonholes. To avoid this, this activity teaches with the shirt on a table, and then buttoned from the bottom to the top. This encourages your child to match up the bottom button with the bottom hole, when fastening a shirt while wearing it.

You will need

- Shirt (or cardigan) with large buttons

1 Place the shirt on the table so your child can see clearly. Open up the shirt, and close it again, so your child can see how it works. Starting at the bottom, slowly guide the bottom button through the first hole.

2 Open up the buttonhole as wide as possible so your child can see that it needs to be open for the button to pass through. Finish the rest of the buttons and then undo them. Pass the shirt over for your child to try.

Other activities to try

Practice with other clothes. Open and close each garment before fastening, and work from bottom to top. Move onto items with smaller buttons.

Choose a large item, such as an adult shirt or cardigan, and teach your child to button while wearing the item.

Try items with snaps and fastenings. Make each movement clear, and follow the same procedure for buttons.

When your child has mastered putting on a shirt or cardigan, help her to learn how to put on a sweater. Choose your own method, but be consistent each time you help.

Check that your child is confident putting on mittens or gloves and other items of clothing.

Fastening a zipper

Children find zippering interesting, but very tricky. You may need to hold the bottom of a zipper while they do the zippering action.

Pants and skirts: Do up the top button, and then do the zipper.

Dresses: Hold the bottom of the zipper before zippering.

Jacket: Put the left end of the zipper into the bottom section and hold securely with the left hand while zippering up with the right hand. If your child is left-handed, this might be tricky at first, so allow plenty of time to practice.

Putting on shoes

If your child is finding it difficult to put on his shoes, teach him how when not wearing them, as explained here. Tying laces is very difficult for a young person so start with Velcro and other fastenings to encourage your child's confidence.

Once your child has mastered these exercises, turn the shoes around with the heels pointing toward him to try. He can then try with the shoes on his feet.

Learning left and right shoes

Before a child starts to fasten his shoes, he needs to identify which goes on which foot. Here are some pointers to help him work it out:

- Hold Velcroed shoes by the straps. The straps should touch back-to-back in the middle.
- Buckled shoes should have buckles on the outside, and not in the middle.
- Write R and L inside rubber boots.
- Save laced shoes until your child is confident with right and left, and dextrous with other fastenings.

Velcroed shoes

1 Ask your child to put the shoes onto a mat on the table with the toe ends facing you.

2 Bring the right shoe forward, lift up the straps, and place them so that your child can see that the straps must match up if they are to hold together. Bring down the left shoe and put back the right shoe. Repeat with the other shoe.

3 Pass the shoes on the mat for your child to try.

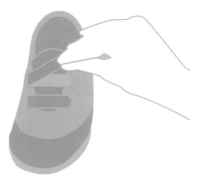

Buckled shoes

1 Ask your child to put the shoes onto a mat on the table with the toes facing you. Starting with the right shoe, lift up the strap and thread it under and up through the buckle.

2 Bend the strap back to reveal the holes. Push the pin into the hole, and finish buckling the shoe.

3 Repeat with the left shoe, but turn it around so the heel is facing you. Unbuckle the shoes and place them on the mat for your child to try.

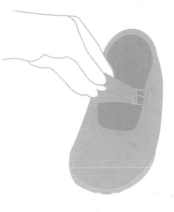

Laced shoes

1 Ask your child to put the shoes onto a mat on the table with the toes facing you. Take the right shoe, and place the laces out to the sides. Cross over the laces.

2 Take the right side lace with your right hand. Cross under the center and pull on both ends to knot.

3 Take the left side lace with your left hand and slide your left hand down until you reach the middle of the lace. Pick it up between your thumb and second finger, and transfer it to your right hand, while your left hand folds the lace in the center to make a rabbit ear.

4 Take the right lace in the right hand, loop over the center section, and pull through to tie a bow.

5 Repeat with the other shoe. Untie both shoelaces and pass the shoes over for your child to try.

Polishing shoes

All children love this activity, and the children I know have often offered to clean my shoes. In their enthusiasm for the task, they have polished the soles, rendering walking a dangerous task! Polishing also helps to develop and refine fine motor skills.

You will need

- Can of neutral-colored polish
- Small container to hold a scoop of polish
- Table knife
- Plastic mat
- Leather child's shoes
- Small shoe brush
- Small cloth
- Tray

1. Before you ask your child to sit down, scoop out a small amount of polish and put it in the container. (This is to limit the amount of polish used.) Spread the mat out on the tray, and add the shoes, polish container, brush, and cloth.

2. Pick up the cloth, take some of the polish and apply it to one shoe. Spread it evenly over the surface.

3. Return the cloth to the tray and pick up the brush. Use a buffing action to shine the shoe.

4. After the activity, you could ask your child why it is that we need to clean our shoes, and why we need to put a mat out to put our shoes on. If he is not sure, guide him to the answer by showing him the bottom of his shoes.

Other activities to try

Try the same activity but polish small wooden objects using furniture polish.

Show your child how to polish a low wooden table.

SAFETY POINT / The use of shoe polish needs to be supervised. If consumed, it could cause acute stomach problems.

Learning to pour

Stop and think how many times you use a pouring action during the day. This uncomplicated movement is easy for an adult but for a child, learning how to pour requires intense concentration and hand–eye coordination. A great way for your child to master this skill is to try pouring beans from one large plastic pitcher to another. Once she is confident doing this, try the same activity using different substances.

You will need

- 2 plastic pitchers
- Package of dried beans or lentils
- Tray

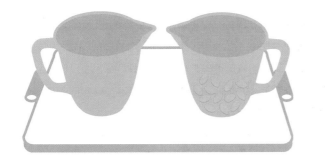

Other activities to try

Replace the beans with finer substances, such as rice or sand.

Try the same activity using water colored with a few drops of food coloring. (You will need a cloth to wipe up any spills.)

Instead of pouring from pitcher to pitcher, try pouring from a pitcher into cups.

Buy a play teaset and add beans, water, etc.

Give your child a pitcher half-filled with water and let her pour the water into glasses for the dinner table.

1 Put the pitchers on the tray with the spouts facing each other and the handles facing out. Fill the pitcher on the right a third full with beans or lentils.

2 Pick up the pitcher on the right with your right hand, supporting it with your left hand, as shown.

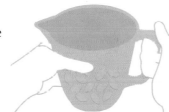

3 Pour the beans into the pitcher on the left. Now reverse the pitchers and invite your child to try the activity.

Learning to transfer

Activities that involve transferring substances, such as spooning and pouring, develop muscular coordination that helps with eating, serving food for oneself and others, and cooking. Such activities also prepare the muscles for the more complex task of writing. As with pouring, this activity begins with a less refined substance moving to a finer substance.

You will need

- 2 small shallow bowls (about the size of a cupcake)
- Teaspoon
- Small tray
- Rice to half-fill one pot

1 Set out the two bowls on the tray with the spoon on the right. Put the rice in the bowl on the left.

Other activities to try

Provide two empty bowls: one each side of the rice bowl. Teach your child to transfer between the two empty bowls.

Replace the rice with finer substances, such as sand or flour.

2 Pick up the spoon and begin to transfer the rice from the left to the right bowl, until the bowl is empty.

3 Reverse the bowls so the bowl with the rice is back on your left, with the spoon on the right. Pass the tray to your child for him to try.

Tip box

■ Always work from left to right. This helps prepare your child for reading.
■ If you take great care when transferring, your child will do the same.
■ If your child is left-handed, hold your spoon in the left hand.

Setting the table

Here is a quick and effective activity that will teach your child how to set the table. Use a sheet of paper with the place setting drawn on it for your child to learn the positions of the cutlery and plate. Once he has mastered this skill, it could become his family job. Many children also enjoy being shown elaborate ways of folding a napkin. As well as the practical benefits, this activity reinforces folding, and right- and left-handed positions.

You will need

- Small plate to fit on the sheet of paper
- Large sheet of thick paper
- Pencil
- Black felt pen
- Table knife
- Fork
- Dessert spoon
- Tray

Before you ask your child to sit down, put the plate in the middle of the paper, and draw around it with the pencil. Follow the same steps for the cutlery, so that you have an outlined place setting on the paper. Go over the pencil outlines in felt pen to make them stand out.

1 Put the sheet of paper onto a tray along with the cutlery and plate. Ask your child to take the tray to the table, and put it in front of him in the middle. Remove the paper and put it in front of the tray.

2 Say to your child, "I am going to match up the plate to the one on the paper." Trace around the rim of the plate with one finger and repeat the action on the paper outline so that your child will see that the shape matches.

3 Say to your child, "Can you match up the cutlery with the outlines on the paper?" Spread the cutlery out on the tray so he can clearly see each item. Encourage him to match up the paper and items.

Other activities to try

Add extra items like a glass or a soupspoon and draw on the outlines. You can also add a napkin, but don't draw on the outline; just show how it folds under the fork.

When your child feels confident about setting the place, get him to take it off the paper. The next stage is to turn the paper over and out of reach, and when he has completed the setting, he can go back and check to see if he was correct.

Learning to use clothespins

This activity is one of the simplest ways to help a child develop muscular coordination. It can be achieved by the youngest children. Once your child has mastered this skill with standard-sized clothespins, she can try this activity using mini or toy clothespins. If you have bought new standard clothespins, use them several times to weaken the spring.

You will need

• Small basket filled with clothespins

SAFETY POINT ⚠ Explain that clothespins are not toys and should not be applied to fingers because they can pinch and hurt.

1 With the basket in front of you, slowly start to attach the clothespins around the basket.

2 Demonstrate the opening and closing action of the clothespin so your child will understand that the clothespin must be fully opened to fit onto the basket and to be taken off again.

Other activities to try

The next time that you are putting out some laundry, give your child some small items of clothing to hang up with clothespins.

3 When you have attached about five clothespins, pass the basket to your child to complete.

4 When she has finished, show her how to remove the clothespins and put them back in the basket.

Using tongs

Children find this activity very appealing because it satisfies their love of sorting and order. In this activity, the emphasis is on the opening and closing action, beginning with large tongs and later refining the action using tweezers. Once your child has mastered this activity you can develop it further by asking him to sort the objects by color or shape.

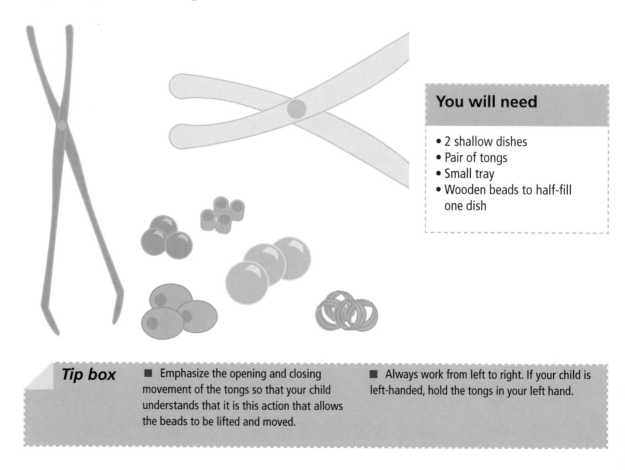

Tip box ■ Emphasize the opening and closing movement of the tongs so that your child understands that it is this action that allows the beads to be lifted and moved.

■ Always work from left to right. If your child is left-handed, hold the tongs in your left hand.

1 Put the dishes on the tray side by side with the tongs on your right. Half-fill the left dish with the beads.

Other activities to try

Provide two or more empty dishes. Teach your child to transfer between the dishes.

Try the same activity but encourage sorting by object, or color, or both.

Use tweezers to transfer dried peas, from eggcup to eggcup. This activity uses the same action as tongs, but as it is a refined action, it is more difficult.

2 Use the tongs (the hand can be held over or under the tongs) to transfer the beads from left to right until the left dish is empty.

3 Switch the dishes so that the dish with the beads is back on the left. Pass the tray over for your child to try.

SAFETY POINT ⚠ Always supervise your child during this activity as small beads can be a choking hazard or can be inserted into the nose or ears.

Opening and closing objects

As a child, one of my favorite toys was a miniature toy safe that had a combination lock with a code that only I knew. Today, the children I teach are equally curious about the opening and closing of objects, from the twisting action of a jam jar lid, to the turning action of a key in a lock. This activity satisfies that curiosity with opening jars and bottles, and later with nuts and bolts, which also refines the turning action.

Choose a wide range of bottles and jars so that your child can clearly see the different sizes of openings and lids.

You will need

- 6 or more small bottles and jars (for example, food coloring bottles and jam jars)
- Basket to hold the bottles and jars

Other activities to try

Use a range of boxes to show a lifting and shutting action.

Use large, loose nuts and bolts to show a more refined turning action. Supervise closely as nuts could be a choking hazard.

Introduce assorted padlocks and keys, and explain what they are used for.

Children are fascinated by keys, but you need to explain the dangers of locking someone in a room, including themselves.

1 Remove the bottles and jars from the basket. Unscrew all the lids and place them in front of the bottles and jars, neatly in a row.

2 Select a lid and go along the row left to right, to find the matching bottle or jar. Emphasize the turning action as you find the right match.

3 Repeat until you have done half the bottles or jars and then invite your child to complete the rest.

4 When she has finished, show her how to unscrew the lids. Be very clear about the different turning actions that are used for opening and closing. When finished, return everything to the basket.

Threading buttons

The activity of threading appeals to all children and is excellent for muscular development and hand–eye coordination. It follows a progression from large buttons with big holes, to small buttons, large beads, and small beads. Once mastered, this skill can be used in jewelry making and other craft projects.

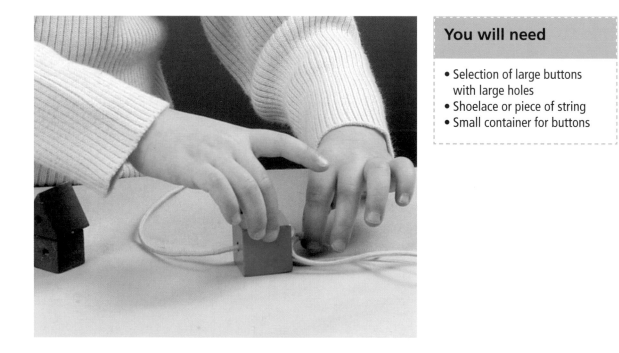

You will need

• Selection of large buttons with large holes
• Shoelace or piece of string
• Small container for buttons

1 Put the buttons and the shoelace or a piece of string in the container.

2 Take the shoelace out of the box. Show and explain to your child that you need to knot the end of the shoelace to stop the buttons from sliding off.

3 Slowly thread the buttons, one by one, all the way to the end of the lace. Show clearly the end of the lace going through the hole, so he understands that this needs to happen for the button to slide down.

4 Thread about six buttons onto the shoelace and then slide them off and put them back in the container, along with the shoelace.

5 Pass the container over for your child to try. When he has completed the threading, he may like to have it tied together to make a necklace.

Other activities to try

Replace the buttons with beads, starting with large beads before progressing to smaller beads.

Try using penne pasta. Afterward, color it by dipping the whole necklace in diluted food coloring.

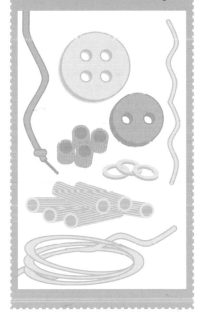

Weaving paper

This activity is an excellent introduction to sewing as it uses the same under-and-over action. By using contrasting colored paper strips, the weaving pattern is emphasized and when complete, your child will have a visual reminder of the action employed. When the mat is finished, display it so that your child can view her achievement.

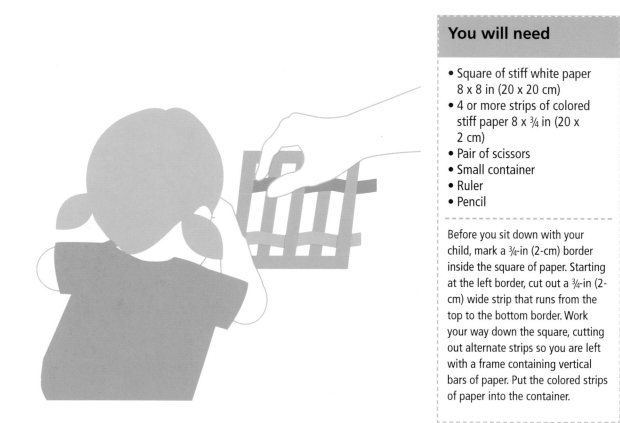

You will need

- Square of stiff white paper 8 x 8 in (20 x 20 cm)
- 4 or more strips of colored stiff paper 8 x ¾ in (20 x 2 cm)
- Pair of scissors
- Small container
- Ruler
- Pencil

Before you sit down with your child, mark a ¾-in (2-cm) border inside the square of paper. Starting at the left border, cut out a ¾-in (2-cm) wide strip that runs from the top to the bottom border. Work your way down the square, cutting out alternate strips so you are left with a frame containing vertical bars of paper. Put the colored strips of paper into the container.

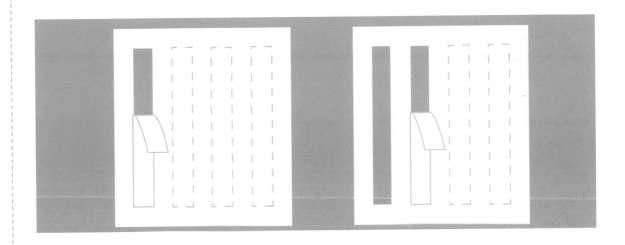

1 With your child seated to the left of you (or right, if left-handed), pick up a strip of paper and start to weave it under then over the paper bars, right to left, until you reach the end.

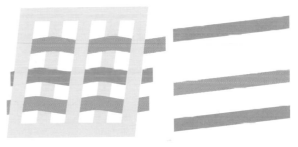

2 Weave two strips of paper and then invite your child to complete the rest. Pull out the paper strips gently if your child wishes to repeat the activity.

Tip box

■ Choose two contrasting colors for the strips of paper so that your child will clearly see the weaving pattern.

■ As you are weaving, push up the strips of paper to keep them in as straight a line as possible.

Sewing cards

In the previous activity, paper was woven in horizontal strips, but in this activity, your child progresses to sewing, using a shoelace, threading it through precut holes around the parameters of sewing cards. Once this skill has been achieved, your child can try sewing with a needle using plastic canvas.

You will need

- Square of cardboard 8 x 8 in (20 x 20 cm)
- Pair of scissors
- Pencil
- Shoelace or piece of string
- Felt pens
- Small tray

SAFETY POINT ! Your child should be aged five or above before he attempts to use a sewing needle. Always supervise closely.

1 Before you sit down with your child, draw an animal shape on the cardboard (make it as large as possible).

2 Cut out the shape, and use the pencil to mark off points for the holes at ¾-in (2-cm) intervals. Cut out holes large enough for the shoelace or string to fit through easily.

3 Ask your child to color in the card, adding a face and animal features. Put the sewing card on a tray along with the shoelace or string.

4 Show your child what happens when you don't make a knot, and then make a knot in the shoelace.

5 Pick up the shoelace with one hand and begin the sewing action. Start with the shoelace above the card, and go under. Then bring the shoelace back up through the next hole.

6 Go about halfway around and then invite your child to complete it. If your child would like to repeat the activity, remove the shoelace carefully.

Other activities to try

Make a whole set of animal sewing cards with your child.

Use plastic canvas or monk's cloth, available from sewing stores. Anything with precut holes is excellent for introducing needle sewing. Show your child how to use a knitting or mending needle, as these are blunt at the end and have a large eye.

Introduce your child to colored threads and stitches such as running stitch and cross-stitch.

Tip box ■ Be consistent in your sewing action; always start from the top and go under, and then up and over to the next hole. ■ Make sure the lace is long enough to go around the whole card.

Cutting with scissors

Most children find that to cut a strip of paper in two is relatively simple, but to cut with care and control is another matter. This activity teaches cutting along a marked straight line, using the scissors carefully, and moving the paper as you cut. It progresses with cutting more difficult lines, and, finally, moving the scissors and paper in different directions.

How to handle scissors

Before learning to cut, children need to learn how to handle scissors safely. Teach your child that when carrying scissors, the scissors need to be held with the whole hand wrapped around the closed blades. Show how to pass the scissors with the handle facing the person.

1 Before you ask your child to sit down, cut the paper into five strips widthwise. Mark a straight line down the center of each strip, using the ruler and felt pen. Put the strips in the container along with the scissors.

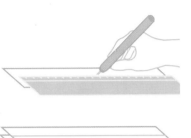

2 Pick up the scissors and show your child how to hold the scissors. (Because of your child's smaller hand size, she will probably prefer to put two fingers into the finger hole.) Show your child the opening and closing action of the scissors.

3 Select a strip of paper and hold it in one hand. Cut slowly, following the line.

4 Move the paper along as you are cutting so she will understand how this helps the cutting process. Exaggerate the opening and closing action so she sees that this needs to happen if the paper is to be cut. Cut another strip.

5 Put the scissors back into the container and give them to your child. Invite your child to finish the rest.

Other activities to try

From cutting straight lines your child can progress to wavy lines and zigzags.

Provide templates to cut out – for example, animals or cars.

Make paper chains. Fold a strip of paper in an accordion fold; draw a person, making sure that the hands and feet are touching the folds. Ask your child to cut out the figure, but not the hands and feet. When she has finished, open the paper to reveal the linked people.

Developing the senses

Young children have heightened senses, and use them fully to expand their knowledge of the world. All the activities in this chapter not only help to stimulate and develop all five senses but also introduce new concepts and vocabulary. The senses become a natural teaching tool, and help to engage your child fully in the activities.

As adults, we tend to use mainly our sight and hearing. When presenting these activities to your child, try to use all your senses, as your child will. In this way, you will begin to appreciate their value for your child's development.

Introducing textural opposites

This very simple activity introduces the terms rough and smooth, using graded sandpaper. Sandpaper is an excellent material for stimulating tactile awareness and for illustrating the textural opposites of rough and smooth. Before the activity starts, your child will need to wash her hands, in order to sensitize her fingers.

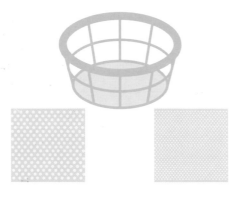

You will need

• Sheet of rough sandpaper
• Sheet of smooth sandpaper
• Container or basket

Cut each sheet of sandpaper into about six pieces and place the pieces in the container or basket.

1 Ask your child to sit on your left (or right, if she is left-handed) and put the basket in front of you. Take out the sandpaper pieces and put them in a row in front of the basket.

2 Say to your child, "I am going to feel the sandpaper and find out if it is rough or smooth."

Tip box ■ Always work from left to right, even if your child is left-handed. This is to prepare her for reading. ■ At this stage, only use the words rough and smooth, not roughest, smoothest, etc. This is to avoid confusion.

3 Beginning at the left, feel across the row of sandpaper pieces using the fingertips of your second and third fingers only. When you find a rough piece, say the word "rough" and place it on your left.

4 Return to the row, and feel to find a piece of smooth sandpaper, and when found say the word "smooth" and put the smooth piece of sandpaper on your right.

5 Pass the two pieces over to your child and invite her to run her fingertips over them in the same way. When she has felt the surfaces, get her to feel them again, but this time say the words "rough" and "smooth" and get her to repeat them.

6 Now pick up the sandpaper pieces and put them in front of you. Sort the rest of the pieces into rough and smooth piles of sandpaper. As you are doing this, say the words "rough" or "smooth" as you feel each piece.

7 Put all the sandpaper in a random order back in the container, and invite your child to sort the sandpaper.

Other activities to try

Introduce two other grades of sandpaper, for example, very rough and very smooth. Repeat the activity, but say, "I am going to feel which is the roughest piece." When found, say, "This is the roughest piece of sandpaper," and place it to one side. Repeat the action, feeling which is the smoothest piece. When you have found it, put it on the right side, with a space in between for the other pieces of sandpaper. Continue until you have a row of graded sandpaper, then invite your child to try the activity.

When your child is happy with this activity, increase the number of pieces to eight.

Word activity

■ Take every opportunity to find surfaces that are rough or smooth, and encourage your child to feel them. For example, say to your child, "I wonder if the bark of that tree is rough or smooth," or "I wonder if that leaf is rough or smooth," or "I wonder which is smoother or rougher, the leaf or the bark?"

Learning tactile opposites

Your child will need to consider the substance of an object, and how this affects the tactile experience. Once this concept is understood, then she will have learned that objects that yield to the touch are "soft" and objects that resist are "hard." As in the previous activities, you start by introducing opposites. Once this concept is learned, you expand on it, so it is important that you follow the steps in order.

You will need

- 6 to 8 small objects that are hard or soft (for example, marbles, wood, play dough)
- Container or basket to put them in

Tip box

■ Choose contrasting objects so your child can clearly feel the difference between hard and soft.

■ Really press your fingers into the object so that your child understands that soft objects yield to the touch.

1 With the basket in front of you and your child to your left (or right, if your child if left-handed), take a hard object out of the basket. Put it on your left. Then take out a soft object, and put it on your right.

2 Press your fingertips into the hard object and say the word "hard." Repeat the action with the soft object and say the word "soft."

3 Pass the two objects over to your child, and invite her to feel the surfaces, as you did.

4 When she has felt the surfaces, get her to feel them again, but this time say the words "hard" and "soft."

5 Invite your child to sort the rest of the objects into hard or soft.

Other activities to try

Show your child how to grade objects from hardest to softest.

Introduce a blindfold so your child grades the objects through touch alone. When showing your child how to do it, say, "I am feeling for the hardest object," and place it to your left. Then say, "I am feeling for the softest object," and continue, comparing with the other objects in the row until you have graded all the objects.

From grading four objects, extend to six to eight objects

Show your child how to sort objects by temperature (coldest to warmest). Choose objects with contrasting temperatures, like cork, marble, wood, stone, and wool.

Try the temperature activity using a blindfold.

Word activity

■ To reinforce the terms hard and soft, ask your child to find a hard or soft object in the room. Then ask her to find two soft, or two hard objects and ask her which is softer or which is harder.

■ Ask your child to find cold or warm objects in the room. You might like to position suitable objects for her to find. Alternatively, ask her to find two cold or warm objects and compare their temperatures.

Comparing textures

Playing with fabrics will expand upon the experiences of the sandpaper activities and teach your child to sort, grade, and match. The sandpaper activities need to be completed before attempting fabric activities because your child will need to have experienced and understood the terms rough, smooth, roughest, and smoothest. This activity follows the same pattern, but uses a blindfold to encourage your child to sort the fabric by "feel," and not by the visual memory of the color and pattern of the fabrics. You will need to read all the steps before you start!

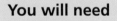

You will need

- 6 pieces of fabric, 4 x 4 in (10 x 10 cm)
- Container for the fabrics
- Blindfold or scarf

Choosing fabrics

Choose contrasting fabrics, such as silk, satin, cotton, corduroy, velvet, wool, and burlap.

1 Arrange the pieces of fabric in a row in front of the basket. Say to your child, "I am going to feel which fabrics are rough and which are smooth, but to make sure I use only my fingers to feel, I am going to cover my eyes." Put on the blindfold.

Tip box ■ If you ask your child a question, give her time to think about it, and give her clues or pointers to help her answer.

2 Feel across the row and select a rough piece of fabric. Feel the fabric, holding it between the thumb and second and third fingers, and make a rubbing action. Feel it again and say "rough." Place it to the left side of the table.

3 Feel the fabrics until you find a smooth fabric; say "smooth" and place it to the right side. Continue until all the fabrics have been sorted into two piles of rough and smooth.

4 Take off the blindfold and put it in the basket. Mix up the fabric pieces, then invite your child to try the activity. You might need to help her put on the blindfold. (Some children can be nervous about putting on a blindfold; if so, ask her to close her eyes instead.)

Other activities to try

When your child is confident with this activity, introduce two or four more pieces of fabric.

Invite her to grade the fabrics from the roughest to the smoothest. Start with four pieces, and work up to eight. You may need to guide your child's hand when she is placing the fabrics in a row. Work from left to right, even if your child is left-handed. This is to prepare her for reading.

Choose three or more different fabrics and cut two squares from each one. Arrange one square of each fabric in a row, and put the other squares in a pile. Ask your child to select matching pieces from each pile.

Introduce materials such as aluminum foil, foam rubber, and cellophane.

Word activity

■ Select a piece of fabric, for example, cotton. Ask your child to find a piece of clothing made from the same fabric. This can lead to looking and feeling the different fabrics of winter and summer clothes and you can discuss why clothes are made from different fabrics. Discuss cotton and wool, so your child can learn the names of two fabrics, and find out their qualities. Aim to teach the names of only two or three fabrics at any one time. If you have velvet cushions or other luxurious fabric cushions, start a conversation with your child about why she thinks it makes a good fabric for a cushion.

The feely bag game

Your child will really enjoy this game, which challenges his memory of touch, pulling together all the tactile experiences that he will have encountered in the previous activities. The aim of the game is to guess by feeling which of the selected objects have been put in the bag. This game can also teach new vocabulary, as you can ask him how he guessed the object in the bag.

You will need

- 3 to 5 different objects, such as favorite toys, apple, etc.
- Drawstring bag (for example, a laundry bag)
- Container or basket for the objects
- Dish towel

Tip box ■ Choose contrasting objects, with different shapes and textures and include some favorite objects, such as toys. ■ For younger children, start off with just three objects, and work up to five.

1 Show your child the objects you have in your container or basket one at a time, and name them.

2 Explain to your child that he is going to have to guess which object you have put into the bag, just by feeling it. Ask your child to turn away and to shut his eyes.

3 Select an object and put it in the bag. Cover up the other objects with the dish towel.

4 Ask your child to open his eyes and pass him the bag. Ask him if he can guess the object in the bag. Give him time to explore the object and if he doesn't seem sure, you could remind him of the objects, for example, "Do you think it is the ball?"

5 When he has guessed correctly, choose another object, and continue until all the objects have been guessed.

Other activity to try

As your child gains confidence in this activity, put two objects, then three into the bag at the same time.

Learning size and shape

This simple activity provides your child with a mathematical experience as it introduces ordering and estimating size and shape to build the blocks into a tower. In addition, mass is introduced. When your child carries the blocks, she will understand that the biggest block is also the heaviest. You also introduce the concept and vocabulary of biggest, smallest, bigger, and smaller.

You will need

- 10 graduated building blocks (ideally, 2 or 3 of the blocks should be big enough to require your child to carry them with both hands)

Tip box

■ Show your child that blocks should be carried one at a time and, when carrying the bigger blocks, to use two hands.

■ Take time to select the block you need. Carry only one block at a time.

■ Be slow and careful in your building of the tower and your child will follow your example.

■ Make sure that you place the blocks in such a way that you get the full graduated effect.

■ When your child has finished building and rebuilding, the blocks need to be put away, to teach your child about being neat.

1 Ask your child to help you take the building blocks to a clear area on the floor.

2 Sit down with your child on your left, and the blocks slightly to your right.

3 Tell your child that you are going to build the blocks into a tower. Select the largest block and put it in front of you in the center, then slowly complete the rest of the tower.

4 Tell your child that you are going to dismantle the tower so that she can build it. Take down the blocks one at a time and place them to the right of your child. (Your child can help you to do this.) Invite your child to build the tower.

Other activities to try

The tower is built again but this time the blocks are placed up one corner rather than centrally.

The blocks are used to build a horizontal stair going left to right, smallest to largest.

Learning height and length

This activity uses paper rods to introduce the concept of length, as your child builds a stair of rods from shortest to the longest. Your child will be required to estimate the length of each rod and where it fits into the stair. You can discuss the same concept by showing photographs of family members and their varying heights; you could even get everyone to line up in a row, from tallest to shortest.

Tip box ■ Make sure the ends of the rods on the left side are lined up straight, so that your child will clearly see the stair effect.

You will need

- Worksheet 1
- Large sheet of paper
- Large sheet of thick cardboard
- Pair of scissors
- Blue and red felt pens
- Glue
- Tray

Color copy, or copy the worksheet onto white paper. Color in the sections red and blue starting with blue for the single section, and then always starting with red from the left side. The first rod will have one section, the second two (one of each color), the third, three sections, and so on. Cut out the rods, stick them onto the cardboard, and cut out, as shown.

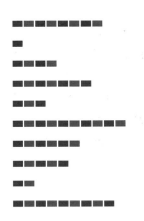

1 Arrange the rods in a random order on a tray, so your child can see them clearly.

2 Put the rods horizontally to the right of you and ask your child to sit on your left.

3 Tell your child that you are going to build the rods into a staircase starting with the shortest. Select the shortest rod and put it in front of you. When you are selecting your rod, run your right hand along to the end so that your child will see that you are finding the next length.

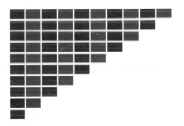

4 Build up the rest of the staircase, finishing with the longest rod.

5 Tell your child that you are going to dismantle the staircase so that she can build it.

6 Take the rods one at a time and place them to the right of your child in a random order. Invite your child to build the staircase.

Word activity ■ Take every opportunity to introduce the mathematical language of long and short. You could ask your child to compare the height of members of the family. Ask, "Who is the shortest?" and "Who is the tallest?"
■ You could also introduce the mathematical language of weight: "heavy" and "light." Ask your child to compare the different weights of food items by using her hands as scales.

Matching two-dimensional shapes

This activity concentrates on the mathematical concept of shape. Your child will learn how to identify a circle and how to estimate the difference between the sizes of the circles. The cut-out circles are matched up to ones drawn on paper. This acts as a control so that your child will be able to see if he has estimated correctly, and to make corrections himself. In "Other activities to try," the activity is repeated with squares and triangles.

1 Ask your child to carry the container to the table, while you take the worksheet. Ask your child to sit on your left with the worksheet in front of you, and the container behind it.

2 Take out the circles and place them in a random order in a row behind the worksheet.

You will need

- Worksheet 2
- Sheets of paper
- Pair of scissors
- Container or basket to hold cut-out circles

Photocopy the worksheet a few times onto stiff paper. Cut out one set of circles and place them in the container or basket. Leave at least one sheet intact.

Tip box   ■ Always work from left to right, even if your child is left-handed. This is to prepare her for reading.

■ Take time when choosing your circles, looking back and forth from the sheet to the paper circles. In this way, your child will see that you are comparing sizes.

3 Tell your child that you are going to match the circles, starting with the biggest and ending with the smallest.

4 Select the biggest paper circle and match it up to the circle on the sheet. Continue until all the circles are matched up.

5 Put the circles back into the container and pass it to your child, along with the worksheet, so he can try.

Other activities to try

On Worksheet 2 you will see two other sections, one with squares and one with triangles. Repeat the activity but matching first the squares, and then the triangles.

Using Worksheet 2, enlarge the sheet onto paper twice. Color the shapes a different color: for example, red circles, blue squares, and yellow triangles. Show your child how to match each shape to the worksheet. Your child may prefer to have the shapes out in the open rather than in the container.

When your child is confident with these games, introduce other shapes such as rectangles, diamonds, and ovals.

Word activity

■ Divide your paper shapes into two equal groups. Hide half around the room and place the other half in the container. Select a shape from the box and say to your child, "Can you find me another circle?" Go through all the shapes until the box is empty.

■ When your child is familiar with the names of the shapes, hide all the shapes and say to your child, "Can you find me a triangle?" Later, you could add, "Can you find me a big square?"

Matching three-dimensional shapes

This activity progresses from the last one, in that the shapes now reappear in 3-D (three-dimensional). The shapes used are familiar objects, which are then given their correct mathematical names, and sorted into pairs. Using familiar objects will help your child to memorize the mathematical names.

You will need

- 2 spheres (for example, tennis balls or marbles)
- 2 cubes (for example, building blocks)
- 2 cylinders (for example, small cans or film canisters)
- Container or basket to put them in

Other activities to try

Increase the number of solids gradually until your child can match six pairs.

You could include other three-dimensional shapes, such as cones, pyramids, and ovoids. You might have toys these shapes, but you could use an ice cream cone and a hard-boiled egg, and show a photograph of a pyramid.

1 Ask your child to carry the container to the table and place it in front of her in the middle. Tell your child that she is going to match up the solid shapes.

2 Say to your child, "Can you find me a building block that is a cube shape?" When she has selected the block, ask her to place it on the left.

3 Ask the same question, but ask for a sphere, and then a cylinder.

4 Ask your child to pair up the solid shapes left in the box, with those on the table.

Word activity

■ You can play the feely bag game (see page 54). Use one sphere, cylinder, and cube. Show each to your child, one at a time, saying its name. Ask your child to close her eyes, while you put one of the solids in the bag. Hide the other two solids and ask your child to open her eyes. Pass the bag to her to feel the solid and try and guess which one it is.

Discovering colors

Children are drawn to color, from colorful objects to magical rainbows. These color activities begin by matching the primary colors, then secondary colors, and finally, grading shades of one color. Use the paint color sample strips that you can find in paint or hardware stores. Choose the brightest primary colors you can find.

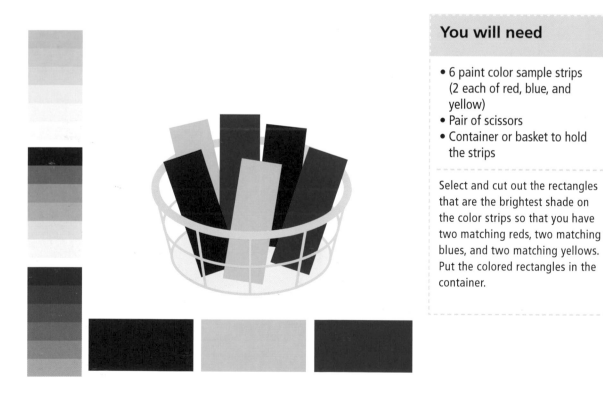

You will need

- 6 paint color sample strips (2 each of red, blue, and yellow)
- Pair of scissors
- Container or basket to hold the strips

Select and cut out the rectangles that are the brightest shade on the color strips so that you have two matching reds, two matching blues, and two matching yellows. Put the colored rectangles in the container.

1 Ask your child to carry the container to the table and to sit on your left.

2 With the container in front of you, remove all the rectangles. Put half of the pieces in a row horizontally, and the other half below in a vertical column.

3 Say to your child that you are going to match up the colors. Start by putting one rectangle of each color in the bottom row, then ask your child to find the matching color to put in the row above, so they are paired up.

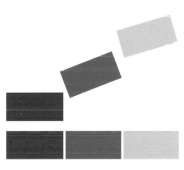

4 Invite your child to finish the matching.

Word activity

■ This activity helps to teach the names of colors. Show your child a red rectangle and say, "Can you find something else in the room that is also red?" Repeat this with other colors, but do only three colors at one time.

■ When your child is confident with the names for different colors, ask him to find objects of certain colors, for example, a red crayon.

Other activities to try

Add more rectangles using the secondary colors of green, orange, and purple.

Progress to matching shades of one color. Cut rectangles from the color strips of the same color shade. Invite your child to match up all the shades of the one color.

Ask your child to arrange the matching colors from the darkest shade at the bottom, to the lightest shade at the top.

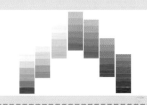

Use seven paint sample color strips and cut out into rectangles to make the colors of the rainbow. Stick them onto a sheet of oak tag in a semicircular shape. Cut out matching rectangles, and invite your child to match up all the colors of the rainbow by placing his rectangles above those on the oak tag rainbow.

Distinguishing sounds

This activity shows your child that when an object is struck, it emits a sound. She will then be asked to consider the quality of the sound and whether it is "loud" or "soft." When she has mastered this skill, the "Other activities to try" includes an option to refine these listening skills, and to grade the sounds from loudest to softest. As with all the activities in this chapter, along with the understanding of the concept comes the language to describe it.

You will need

- 4 to 6 objects that make a loud or soft sound (for example, 2 pan lids banged together, or a jar of coffee to shake)
- Large tray to carry the objects

Tip box

■ Keep the language you use brief and to the point. If you overburden your child with language, the actual aim of the activity will be lost.

■ Take time to compare the sounds so that your child will understand that you need to listen carefully to make a choice of what type of sound it is.

■ I would not suggest that you use musical instruments in this project, as they could distract from the activity.

1 Ask your child to sit on your left with the tray in front of you.

2 Tell your child, "We are going to listen to the sounds these objects make, and decide whether it is a loud or soft sound."

3 Select an object that you know makes a loud sound. Make its sound and then say the word "loud" and place it on the left. Repeat with an object with a soft sound and place it on the right.

4 Hand your child the objects and invite her to sort the rest of the sounds into soft sounds and loud sounds.

Other activities to try

Add extra objects with sounds. Work up until you have ten sounds.

Ask your child to sort the sounds from the loudest to the softest. Work with four to five sounds. Start by identifying the object with the loudest sound, then the one with the softest sound. Invite your child to finish the grading.

Word activity

■ When you are out with your child, encourage her to listen to the sounds around her. Ask her questions about the sounds she hears. For example, "Is the sound your feet make on the pavement loud or soft?" Or you could compare sounds by saying, "Which sound is the loudest?"

Feature

■ If your child experiences any difficulty in achieving these auditory activities (in particular, matching sounds), you might need to have her hearing checked. Hearing problems in young children are quite common. If your child is suffering from a cold, this can reduce hearing for a short period.

Comparing sounds

Your child has learned how to compare different levels of sounds and to grade them from the loudest to the softest. Here, listening skills are refined as your child tries to match sounds. This might sound easy, but it requires careful listening and concentration. There are no visual aids, and she must rely entirely on memory of the sound until she listens to the next one.

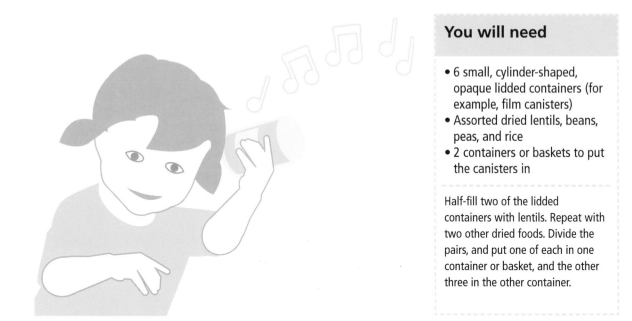

You will need

- 6 small, cylinder-shaped, opaque lidded containers (for example, film canisters)
- Assorted dried lentils, beans, peas, and rice
- 2 containers or baskets to put the canisters in

Half-fill two of the lidded containers with lentils. Repeat with two other dried foods. Divide the pairs, and put one of each in one container or basket, and the other three in the other container.

Tip box ■ When teaching your child to listen to quiet sounds, you might like to show her how to listen carefully by listening close to one ear. Teach her this by always using the same ear to listen to the sounds. To help you remember, pick up the canisters with your right hand, and then you will automatically listen with the right ear.

1 Ask your child to carry one container or basket, while you carry the other to the table.

2 Invite your child to sit on your left and put one container on your left and the other on your right toward the back of the table. Take the canisters out of the containers and place them in front of you.

Other activity to try

Increase the number of canisters until your child is matching up to six pairs of sounds. You could use sugar, coffee, and breakfast cereal in the canisters, for new sounds.

3 Say to your child, "I am going to match and pair up the different sounds." Pick up a canister from the left side, with your right hand, and shake to listen.

4 Pick up a canister from the right side, with your right hand, and shake to listen.

5 Go back to the first canister to check if it matches the sound. Keep trying the canisters on the right side until you find the matching sound. When you do, pair the canisters and put them in front of you, starting at the left. Continue until all the canisters are matched.

6 Invite your child to match and pair the sounds. Set out the canisters, ready for your child to try the activity. Afterward, you might like to open the canisters to check that she was right.

Musical scales

The previous activities have dealt with contrasting, comparing, grading, and matching sounds. In this next activity, the harmonics of sound are introduced by making a musical scale from bottles filled with different levels of water. Your child will also be introduced to high and low sounds, and the idea that the harmonics of sound work only in a certain order.

You will need

- 5 glass bottles or glasses
- Water
- Teaspoon
- Food coloring (optional)

Color the water first, to add interest to the activity. Fill the bottles or glasses with different levels of water to make a scale of sounds. Tap each with the teaspoon to check for a contrasting sound. If you need to make more of a contrast between the sounds, adjust the amount of water in the bottles.

SAFETY POINT ! Explain to your child the dangers of broken glass. Let him see you handling and carrying with care, and he will learn to do the same.

Other activities to try

From making a scale using four bottles, progress to eight, which is the number in a full musical scale.

1 Show your child how to carry a bottle or glass, one by one, safely to the table, with one hand on the base and one on the side.

2 With your child on your left, put the bottles in front of you in a row, toward the back of the table.

If your child comments on the different bottle sizes or the water in them making a difference in the pitch of the sounds, let him experiment with these ideas.

3 Say to him, "I am going to show you how to make a musical scale. First I need to listen to find the lowest sound." Pick up the spoon and gently tap the sides of the bottles or glasses to find the lowest sound. When you have found the right bottle, take it out of the row and put it on the left.

4 Say to him, "Now I need to listen to find the highest sound." Repeat the action and select the highest sound and put the bottle on the right, leaving a space for the other three bottles.

5 Invite your child to complete the scale, saying, "I have found the bottle with the lowest sound [tap the bottle] and the one with the highest sound [tap the bottle]. Now, can you put in order the sounds that come in between?" Set the bottles up in front of your child so that he can complete the scale.

Contrasting smells

Children will always comment on the smells around them, so your child will enjoy this activity. It requires her to sort various smells into pleasant and unpleasant ones. As with all the activities in this chapter, you begin by introducing opposites. This activity will also give your child the opportunity to increase her vocabulary to describe different smells.

You will need

- 6 items with contrasting smells, for example, perfume, flowers, citrus fruits, coffee, and vinegar (don't use household cleaning products, as they can be harmful when inhaled)
- 6 small containers, for example, jars with lids or film canisters
- Absorbent cotton pads or balls
- Tray

Soak each cotton pad with a different smell. Put each cotton pad in a separate container and cover with a lid, plastic wrap, or aluminum foil. Leave the containers for about 5 minutes so that the smell infuses the absorbent cotton. Select one jar with a pleasant smell and put it on the front right-hand corner of the tray and then select a jar with an unpleasant smell and put it on the front left-hand corner. Put the rest of the jars at the back of the tray.

SAFETY POINT ! While you want your child to explore the smells around her, make her aware that certain substances give off fumes. Toxic household products should not be used for this project, and should be locked away safely at all times.

Other activities to try

Increase the number of smells from six to eight.

Play a game matching smells, using two sets of containers, each containing matching pairs of smells. Place one of each at either end of a tray, and show your child how to recognize a matching smell.

Play a game of guessing the smell. Go through each canister, smelling with your child, and tell her the name of the smell. Now ask her to smell one canister, and to guess the smell. If she needs help, ask questions, such as, "Is it the lemon?" Work through all the canisters.

1 Ask your child to sit on your left, and put the tray in front of you in the middle. Tell your child that you are going to sort the smells into pleasant and unpleasant smells.

2 Pick up the jar on the right-hand side with the pleasant smell, open it, smell it, and say something like, "That's a very nice smell," and then put it on the right side of the table. Show your child you are taking your time smelling before deciding what kind of smell it is.

3 Repeat with the jar with the unpleasant smell and say something like, "I don't like that smell; it's nasty." Put the jar on the left side of the table.

4 Invite your child to finish sorting the smells so that she finishes with the unpleasant smells on the left and the pleasant smells on the right.

5 Set up the jars in exactly the same way in front of your child, for her to try the whole activity.

Word activity

■ When you are out with your child in the yard or the park, take time to explore the smells to be found there. Expand on the terms nice and nasty to fragrant, smoky, lemony, or salty. Always give your child time to experience the smells and comment on what she thinks about them.

■ Explain that not everyone likes the same smells, for example, some people like the smell of garlic, and others don't. Ask your child what her favorite smell is, and why.

Identifying tastes

In this activity, your child will discover that while every food has its own flavor, it also has an overriding quality of sweetness, sourness, or saltiness. He will sort the food into three sets, and to isolate the taste, the activity is done blindfolded. You may think that your child will be unwilling to try foods blindfolded, but I have found that once children see an adult doing this, they are reassured.

You will need

- 3 foods, one each that is sweet, sour, or salty (for example, an apple, a lemon, and salty potato chips)
- 3 small dishes
- Paper towels
- Tray
- Blindfold

Slice the food into bite-sized pieces. Put each food onto one of the dishes and place on the tray. Place the paper towels alongside on the tray.

1 Ask your child to sit to your left and have the tray in front of you with the paper towel closest to you. For this activity, the work area will be on the tray.

2 Tell him, "I am going to taste the food and see if it tastes salty, sour, or sweet, but I only want to taste with my tongue, and not look with my eyes."

3 Put on the blindfold. Select a food; if it tastes salty, it goes on the paper on the left. The sour food goes in the middle, and the sweet on the right. As you are tasting each food, say, "This tastes salty [or sour or sweet]." Continue until all the foods have been tasted.

4 Remove the blindfold and invite your child to sort the food. If there are some foods that he is not familiar with or is reluctant to try, suggest that he lick the food or take a "fairy" bite. If he is very happy with the food, allow him to eat it, and then ask him to take another piece to put on the paper.

Other activities to try

Change some of the foods and increase the number of foods tasted from five to eight.

Play "Guess the food." Use three or four foods, such as slices of fruit, chips, or cubes of cheese. Let your child try each food, and then say, "Now guess the food, tasting only with your tongue, and not looking with your eyes. You will need to wear a blindfold." After he has tasted the food, ask him to guess what food he has just tasted. If he is having difficulty remembering, go through the names of the foods to stimulate his memory.

Try this game using both familiar and not so familiar foods. You can also aim to increase the number of foods tasted to five.

Tip box
- Choose foods with clearly defined tastes of salty, sour, and sweet.
- When your child is doing the activity, you may need to guide his hand to the dishes.
- If he eats all of the food, remind him to take another piece to put on the paper.

Language development

Children approach language in a different way
than adults. If your child is enjoying an activity,
he will "absorb" the language being introduced;
it will not seem like hard work. The activities in
this chapter will help to instill in your child a love
of language and books, and when you achieve this,
reading will follow naturally. There is no one set
formula for developing your child's interest in
language. It may develop through an interest in
stories, poems, or songs, or in finding out about
a favorite topic. The activities include some of each
of these, and will provide an excellent introduction
to the world of language.

Learning to love books

Just as your child has learned to care for and respect the materials used in other activities, the same lessons need to be applied to books.

Before your child handles any books, check his hands to see that they are clean. Show your child that pages can get torn if they are not turned with care by demonstrating on a scrap piece of paper. Explain that books are not to be marked or drawn on and need to be returned to the shelf or box when finished. Remember, you are the role model; if your child sees you taking care of books, then he will do the same. If you have books that you have kept from your childhood, show them to your child, explaining why you love the books and why you have looked after them.

For a younger child, I would recommend having a book box, so he can choose easily. To help your child with returning books, make sure that the box or shelves are accessible and are not too tightly packed. You could show an older child how to put a book back on a shelf by pushing back other books and slipping it in. Also show him how to organize his books – for example, with one shelf for fiction and the other for nonfiction.

Selecting books

With such a multitude of books to choose from, where do you begin? Here are some guidelines to help you make your selection:

- When you go to the bookstore or library, allow yourself as much time as possible.
- Whenever possible, take your child, so that he can experience the pleasure of browsing through books.
- If you are choosing a book for your child to look at, choose one suitable for his age level. When selecting a book for story-telling, select one aimed about a year and a half above your child's age.
- Choose a mixture of short and long stories, and as your child gets older, he could have a longer bedtime book, with a chapter that is read every night.
- Check to see if the book has any images or ideas that may frighten him; this is especially important if it is a book for bedtime. Avoid just glancing at the first two pages; you might be surprised by an unexpected ending.
- Choose books that you know your child has an interest in, such as animals or transportation. Also consider books that deal with issues such as feelings, sharing, and friendship.
- Make sure that there is a balance of books between the fantastical and the everyday, with a wide range of human emotions.
- Nonfiction books are great for dealing with "first-time situations," such as a new baby in the family, going to the doctor, or the first day at school. They can also be used to explore an interest your child may have – for example, dinosaurs – or answer questions about the world around him.
- Choose books that contain clear illustrations that illuminate the text and, in the case of fiction, give an idea of the sequence of the story.
- Finally, and very important, allow your child to have some input into the selection.

Reading to your child

"Are you sitting comfortably? Then I'll begin." That's the way all stories should start, because our enjoyment of a story is increased if we are comfortable and ready to listen. Set aside a time for storytelling, and make sure that when you are reading to your child, he is comfortable and ready. Think about creating a reading corner in his bedroom, with floor cushions and a soft blanket for winter. Check that he can see the book and, more important, the pictures.

- How a story is read affects how your child follows and understands it. I suggest that you read the story first. This enables you to check for suitability, but also so you can introduce it, to draw your child in before it starts. For example: "This is my favorite story because . . ." or "This story makes me laugh because . . ." Or, you can tell him about the beginning of the story: "In this story, a little mouse goes on an adventure; let's see what happens."

- With some stories, you may need to reassure your child if you think there could be parts that he could find a little scary. For example, in *The Three Billy Goats Gruff*, you could explain that trolls exist only in storybooks. For older children you could say, "This story is about three billy goats and a troll, but I think the billy goats are going to be smarter; let's find out."

- During the story, ask questions and make comments. If you know that the story is reaching a very exciting part, pause before it to ask your child the possible outcome; for example, "Do you think the little boy is going to be rescued?" If the story is dealing with a childhood issue, for example, sharing, you could make a comment on the situation: "That wasn't very nice of the little girl not to share her toys." By questioning and commenting in this way, your child will want to do the same. Be careful that the questions and comments don't get in the way of the sequence of the story. If you fear that this may be happening, say to your child, "Let's continue the story, and we can think about the question when the story is finished." When the story is finished, take time to talk through with your child what he thought about the story, and any issues arising from it.

The end

Enjoying word play

Through your storytelling, you have enabled your child to experience the potential excitement of language. Now you can help her to explore the vocal power of words through their sounds, rhythms, and rhymes.

Nursery rhymes

- The appeal of nursery rhymes is universal; such is the influence of them in our childhood, that we remember them as adults. The fact that your child will not understand the original meaning of the rhyme will not deter his enjoyment of it. Part of the appeal of nursery rhymes is the sheer nonsense of the images: Humpty Dumpty on the wall or mice running up a clock, for example.

- Nursery rhymes will introduce your child to words that rhyme, and children find this a very exciting aspect of language. You can extend upon this by looking at the rhyming words in the rhymes, seeing if you can add to them or make a nonsense sentence from them.

- Children also very much enjoy nursery rhymes with actions; not only does this help them to remember the rhyme, but it develops their coordination. To make your child aware of the rhythms in the words, try saying the rhyme with your child to a clapping beat.

Poetry

- The rhymes and play on words in poetry are more intricate than in nursery rhymes. Like stories, poetry can give children a wider understanding of the world around them, and help them deal with childhood experiences. But unlike stories, the experience is more intense and concentrated. In *The Cat in The Hat*, children love the absurdity of the images that are created by the play on the words. Also, they enjoy the poem because they know that the story is fantastical. Poems and rhymes can also be used as a memory aid for learning topics such as days of the week or months of the year.

- Children enjoy learning poetry by heart, and take great pride when they manage to memorize a poem. Start with a poem no more than four lines long, and work up to something longer. Your objective should be to foster an enjoyment of language, not to concentrate on the mechanics of learning it. Never spend longer than ten minutes at a time on learning a poem.

- As well as memorizing poetry, you could also introduce some tongue twisters, such as "Peter Piper."

Making up stories

- By helping your child to make up her own stories, you will be helping her to understand how a story is constructed. Begin by discussing with your child the characters in the story, what their names are, and where they live. Then give ideas as to what might happen to the characters, for example, "Do they have an adventure?" Tell the story, but stop often to ask your child, "What happens next?" When the story is finished, comment on the ideas that she has used in the story, for example, "That was a really good idea to have the grandfather come to the rescue of the children."

The phonetic alphabet

In Montessori, the phonetic sounds of the alphabet are always taught before the names of the letters in the alphabet. As well as teaching the phonetic sound of the letter, we also teach how to trace the letter, in the same direction as you would write it.

This activity uses salt trays because children respond to the tactile feel of the salt, helping them to memorize the tracing direction for that letter. Montessori schools use sandpaper letters; if you are feeling very industrious, you could make your own set of sandpaper letters, using the letters on Worksheet 4 as a guide. Trace around them, cut them out, and stick them onto thick cardboard.

You will need

- 2 small baking sheets 9 x 13 in (23 x 33 cm)
- Salt to half-fill the trays
- Worksheet 3, alphabet letters with phonetic sounds

1 Make sure that your child has clean and dry hands for this activity. Ask your child to carry one of the trays to the table, while you carry the other. With your child on your left, put one of the trays in front of her, and the

Tip box

- Don't be tempted to skip any of the stages.
- Try to encourage your child to say the phonetic sound while tracing the letter.

- Introduce only two letters at one time. Choose letters that sound very different, in both written form and in phonetic sound.
- If your child is unable to name any letter sound, go back to an earlier stage.

other on your right. (The trays need to be turned horizontally.)

2 Trace the letter "a" using the full width of the tray to form the letter, and using your index finger. Say its phonetic sound (use the worksheet for reference). Pass the tray to your child to trace over the letter, and as she is doing this, say, "This is 'a'."

3 Switch the trays and repeat the same steps for "t." Repeat the same steps again for both letters, to reinforce the work.

4 Put both trays in front of your child, and ask her, "Can you show me the 'a' and can you show me the 't'?"

5 Then switch the trays around, but this time say, "Can you trace the 'a' and can you trace the 't'?" Then ask, "Which one is the 'a' and which is the 't'? Can you trace it?"

6 Point to the "a" tray and ask, "What is this?" After your child has named it, ask her to say the sound again and to trace the letter. Point to the "t" tray and follow the same steps.

7 Repeat for a second time, but start with the "t."

Other activities to try

Continue introducing the rest of the phonetic alphabet, but always review the two letters from the previous time. Keep a record of the letters you have covered.

Collect three or four small objects all beginning with the same phonetic sound, for example, bear, ball, and box. Place them on a tray along with five objects beginning with a mixture of different phonetic sounds. Ask your child to carry the tray to the table. Now ask her to pick out those objects beginning with your chosen sound. You may need to pick up each object, ask your child what it is, and then ask what its initial sound is.

Ask your child to remove objects from the tray, leaving behind those objects beginning with the chosen sound.

Choose two or three objects starting with different phonetic sounds and ask your child to sort them into phonetic sound groups. To help her, ask questions: for example, "Which objects start with a 'b' sound?"

Identifying letters

These next two activities focus on the written symbols for different letters. In this first activity, you will use a salt tray to write a letter, which then has to be matched to paper letters. As your child becomes more confident identifying letters, you will introduce more letters to choose from.

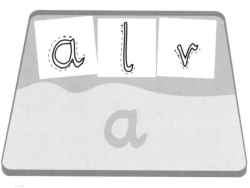

1 Ask your child to carry the basket to the table, while you carry the salt tray. Put the salt tray in front of him and the basket in front of you.

2 Select three letters from the basket, making sure that they contrast in form to each other. Put the letters in a row above the salt. Trace one of the letters in the salt. Ask your child to go over your tracing, and then to select the paper letter that matches it.

3 Ask your child to rub the letter from the salt while you select another three letters. Repeat the same steps until you have gone through about eight letters.

You will need

- Worksheet 4
- Basket or container
- Baking sheet 9 x 13 in (23 x 33 cm)
- Salt to half-fill tray

Photocopy the sheet, and cut out the letters along the dotted lines. Put the individual letters into the basket or container and half-fill the baking tray with salt.

Other activity to try

Increase the number of paper letters selected from three to six.

Matching paper letters

In this activity, two sets of paper letters are used. In the previous activity, only one pair of letters was matched up; this is now increased to three pairs, then six, and finally eight.

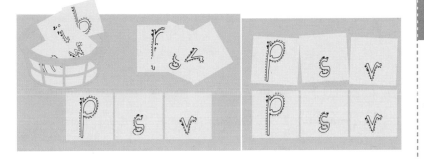

You will need

- Worksheet 4
- Pair of scissors
- 2 small baskets or containers

Photocopy another set of letters, then put each set of letters in a basket or container.

1 Ask your child to take one of the baskets to the table, while you take the other. Ask your child to sit on your left. Put one of the baskets in front of him, toward the back, and the other basket in front of you.

2 Ask your child to take three letters out of his basket and put them in a row at the front. Find the same three letters from your basket and put them in a pile in front of your child.

3 Ask your child to match up the letters, until all three letters have been paired. Put the paired letters in one pile to the right of you. When the activity is finished, you will need to separate the letters back into the two alphabets.

Other activities to try

From pairing and matching three pairs, increase this to six, then to eight pairs.

Arrange one set of paper letters in rows, in alphabetical order, on a large tray. Put the other set in a basket. Ask your child to take a letter out of the basket and pair it up with the one on the tray. You may need to give some clues, such as, "I think you will need to look in the top row."

Word building

This activity is an essential step toward the final goal of reading. Through listening to the phonetic sounds, your child will build words aurally and visually.

You will need

- Worksheet 4
- Worksheet 5
- Pair of scissors
- 2 envelopes
- Large tray
- Ticky tack

Photocopy Worksheet 4 five times (if you have some alphabet letters from the previous activities they can be reused). Stick one sheet onto the tray using ticky tack, and cut the rest of them up into individual letters. Put the letters in piles onto the tray to match the alphabet sheet.

Photocopy Worksheet 5. Cut out the words and pictures and put them into phonetic sound groups. Put each group in a separate envelope. Choose one envelope at a time for the activity. Use the pictures first; the words are used later.

1 Ask your child to take one envelope to the floor while you carry the tray. Work on a carpeted area but make sure it is not patterned, as this can be distracting. Ask your child to sit on your left, putting the tray in front of him. Place the envelope in front of you.

2 Take three pictures from the envelope, and put them in front of your child. Ask your child to choose one of the

Tip box ■ This is an activity that demands careful listening to the individual sounds of the word, so take time to sound the words, slowly and clearly.
■ For some children, "building" two words is as much as they can cope with the first time they attempt this activity.
■ If your child chooses an incorrect sound, just say, "Let's listen again." Similarly, if he puts a letter the wrong way around, nothing needs to be said, as he will discover this when he compares the letters using the word cards.

pictures, for example, "pig." Say to your child, "We are going to build the word 'pig' using the letters." Ask him to put the picture on his left, just below the tray.

3 Now say, "What is the first sound you can hear when I say the word 'pig'?" Get him to say the word with you several times, with each phonetic sound spoken slowly and clearly. Help him to put an emphasis on the first sound only.

4 When he says "p", ask him to find the "p" letter from the alphabet tray and put the letter next to the picture.

5 Now say to your child, "We have the 'p' but now we need to listen for the next sound." Repeat the same steps as before, to find the "i," placing it next to the "p." Your child may go straight to the end sound of "g" (children find it much easier to hear the beginning and end sounds in words). If this happens, follow the same steps, but when he puts the letter "g" next to "p," ask him to leave a space. Tell him that he needs to listen to find another letter to go between the "p" and "g."

6 Ask your child, "Can you listen for the last sound in pig?" Follow the same steps until the "g" letter is found and put next to the "p" and the "i" to make "pig."

Other activities to try

Repeat with a second and third word from the same vowel group. Use words with three letters, for example, "tin" and "pip."

When your child has completed three words, ask him if he would like to build a fourth word. Gradually build this to six words, but only increase the number at his pace.

When your child has completed one vowel group, go onto another one. Because it will be a new vowel sound, work with him for the first one or two words and then let him complete the whole six.

Introduce four-letter phonetic words. You could prepare the word and picture worksheet for this, following the pattern of Worksheet 5.

Reading using word and picture cards

The same picture cards that were used in the previous activity are used again, but this time they help to decode the written word. Your child will need to have completed the previous activity before attempting to read the cards.

pig

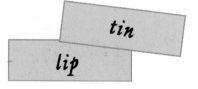

tin

lip

Tip box   ■ Encourage your child to say the words out loud with you. Get a little faster each time, so he hears the blending of the sounds.   At the same time, he needs to look at the pictures so that he begins to understand how the pictures will help to make sense of the words.

1 Choose one group of picture and word cards (for example, words all using the same vowel in them), and ask your child to take the envelope to the table, and to sit on your left.

2 Take out three pictures and ask your child to put them in a row in front of him in the middle of the table. While he is doing that, find the matching word cards and put them together in a pile in front of your child.

3 Ask your child to read the first word. He will need to go slowly through the individual sounds. Ask him what the first sound of the word is. Tell him to look for a picture that begins with that sound, and if necessary, take him through each of the pictures, asking him to tell you its first sound. When he has read the word, ask him to put it under the picture.

4 Follow the same steps until all the word cards are read and there is a row of pictures with their words underneath. If your child is stuck on one of the words, say to him, "We will come back to this word." Put the word on the bottom of the pile so it can be attempted again at the end.

Other activities to try

When your child is confident matching the words with the pictures, increase the number of pictures to six. Ask him to set the picture cards out in two rows of three. You can use the previous three cards again, as it is good to have a mixture of the familiar with the new. Sit with your child until he has read and completed the first or second picture card, and then say you will return in five minutes to see how he is doing. When you return, ask him to read the words, and to say each sound that makes up the word.

Let your child work through the other vowel groups. Now that he understands the activity, he can read six cards at once. As before, sit with him until he has completed the first or second card, and then say you will return in five minutes to see how he is doing. When you return, ask him to read the words, and to say each sound that makes up the word.

Constructing phrases

Your child will enjoy this activity because the phrase that he constructs can be as nonsensical as he wishes. Through the word-building activities, your child will have learned to construct and read three- and four-letter phonetic words. This activity shows how to use these words in the context of a phrase and then in a sentence. It also introduces sight words, a word that cannot be "sounded" but must be learned by sight, for example, "the."

The	sun	sat
A	tin	jumps
	cat	hops
		digs
		runs
		put

You will need

- Worksheet 6
- Set of three-letter picture and word cards from Worksheet 5
- Pair of scissors
- 3 envelopes
- Colored pencils

Photocopy Worksheet 6 twice, and shade each column a different color: blue for the articles and yellow for the verbs. Shade lightly, so as not to obscure the word. Cut out the words and put them in separate envelopes from the pictures.

1 Put the envelope on the tray. Ask your child to take the tray to the table and to sit on your left. With the tray in front of your child in the middle, ask him to choose three picture cards from the picture envelope and put them in a row in front of him.

Tip box ■ Keep the noun, picture, and word cards in separate envelopes.

■ Follow the same order of words, starting with the noun, then the verb (describe it as a "doing" word), followed by "the" or "a."

Other activity to try

When your child can construct three phrases, use three other picture cards in that group. Continue with the rest of the vowel groups, and finally move on to the four-letter words, always working in groups of three.

2 Take out the verbs and the two "the" cards, and arrange them on the tray in vertical columns. Add the three noun cards that match the pictures your child has chosen. Put the envelopes to your right.

3 Ask your child to choose one of the pictures and put it just below the tray in the middle. Ask him to identify the picture, and to find the matching word on the tray. (You will need to point out to him where the column of nouns is.) Ask him to place it under the picture.

4 Ask your child to choose what the word is doing. For example, if he chose "cat," ask what the cat could be doing. Show him the column of verbs to read through with your guidance. Ask him to select one, and put it after the noun. Follow the same steps for the other two pictures.

5 Return to the first picture, and explain that all naming words need to have "the" or "a" before it. Go on to give an example, such as, "The frog hops." Ask your child to choose "the" or "a" for his sentence. (At this stage, do not worry about teaching the correct context for using "the" or "a.") Follow the same steps to add "the" or "a" to the other two phrases.

Making a sentence

When your child is confident constructing a phrase, he can try building the phrase into a sentence. In this activity, he will add an adjective, preposition, second article, and second noun. Part of the enjoyment of this activity is that your child can construct sentences as nonsensical as he wishes; there is no need for the sentence to make sense. This is a difficult activity, so when your child has completed it, let him know what a good job he has done.

You will need

- Paper
- Black felt pen
- All the word cards from Worksheet 5 and Worksheet 6

Tip box

■ Wait until your child is fully confident in one stage of this activity before introducing a new concept.

■ While working, keep each part of the sentence separate from the others, to avoid confusion.

■ Remember that the sentences don't have to make complete sense at this stage; the point is to understand the meaning of "sentence."

1 Follow the same steps as on the previous activity, but this time, add adjectives to the phrases. Tell your child that he is "describing" words. Leave a space between "the" or "a" and the noun, and say, "We are going to add a new word that describes our [for example] cat."

The red cat sat

2 Follow the same steps, but this time add prepositions to the phrases. After your child has added the adjectives, say, "We are going to add a new word that tells you where [for example] the cat sat."

The red cat sat on

3 Follow the same steps, but this time add a second noun. After your child has added the prepositions, say, "We are going to add a new word that tells us what [for example] our cat sat on." Leave a space between the preposition and the noun.

The red cat sat on log

4 Follow the same steps, but this time, add a second "the" or an "a." After your child has added the noun, he might realize why a space has been left before it. If not, point to the first noun and "the" or "a" before it. Remind your child that he needs "the" or "a."

The red cat sat on the log

5 When your child has finished, explain that he has made a sentence and review all the steps he went through. Maybe add a paper dot to represent the period. Complete the other two phrases into sentences.

The red cat sat on the log.

Making a diary

Creating a diary is a very good way for children to understand the idea of sequence. You could save this activity until you are on vacation, or simply record the events of a normal week.

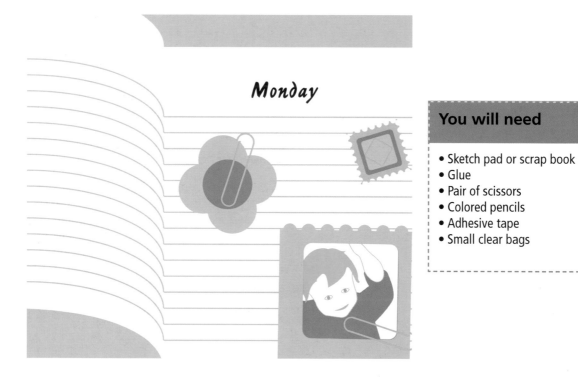

Monday

You will need

- Sketch pad or scrap book
- Glue
- Pair of scissors
- Colored pencils
- Adhesive tape
- Small clear bags

1. On the first page, print "My Diary." If your child is old enough, he could print it himself. Print the day, and the date at the top of each page to make a full week.

2. Each day, help your child to gather and collect items that he could put in his diary, for example, postcards, shells, leaves, feathers, flowers, wrappers, tickets, and photographs.

3. Encourage your child to put the item in the diary on the day it happens or he may forget on which day he collected each item. Put items such as shells or feathers in small clear bags, and tape or staple them in. If there was a day when nothing was collected, your child could draw a picture of what he did that day.

4. Older children should be encouraged to write a sentence or two underneath each item or picture to describe it. When the diary is complete, review it with your child, going through each day to see if he can remember what happened. This is not a test for your child, so give him time to look at the pictures or items before he comments.

Making a book

The most obvious way for your child to understand how a story is constructed is to make a book. This activity uses the "story" of the life cycle of the butterfly, because it has a natural progression. Before your child makes his book, he will need to be familiar with the life cycle. One of the best ways to do this is to buy caterpillar eggs by mail, complete with the correct food and environment. If this is not possible, a good book on butterflies will show the different stages of the cycle.

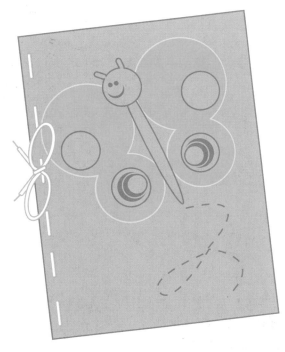

You will need

- Sheets of white paper
- Ruler
- Pencil
- Colored pencils or felt pens
- Book about the life cycle of the butterfly
- Hole punch
- String or ribbon

Using your ruler and pencil, divide the paper into six equal squares.

1 Tell your child that he is going to make his own book about the life cycle of the butterfly. Help him to draw a different stage of the cycle in each square.

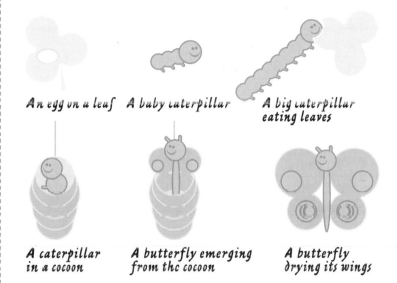

An egg on a leaf   *A baby caterpillar*   *A big caterpillar eating leaves*

A caterpillar in a cocoon   *A butterfly emerging from the cocoon*   *A butterfly drying its wings*

2 Ask your child to shade in and cut out the pictures and to stick one on each page.

3 If your child is old enough, encourage him to write a sentence or two about each picture.

4 Provide another sheet of paper or oak tag to make a front cover. Hole-punch each sheet of paper, and show your child how to put the whole book together with a piece of string. Ask your child to decorate the cover.

Other activities to try

Eric Carle's *The Very Hungry Caterpillar* is a fictional account of the life cycle of the butterfly. The caterpillar eats its way through an assortment of food, including lollipops and cheese. Your child could change this to foods of his own choosing. He might also like to add holes to his book.

Rod Campbell's *Dear Zoo* features a zoo that keeps sending people the "wrong" animal for a pet, until finally they send an animal that is "just right." Your child could change the animals to suit him. He might like to add flaps to the cover of his book, too.

Creating a family tree

Through the experience of creating a family tree, your child will learn about where he fits into his family, and come to understand the terms past, present, and future.

1 On the large sheet of colored paper, ask your child to draw a large tree to fill the whole page. Tell your child that he is going to make a family tree.

2 On one white sheet of paper, ask your child to draw a picture of each family member, or to find photographs.

3 Help your child to stick the pictures or photographs onto the tree, with the grandparents at the top, parents in the middle, and children at the bottom. You may also like to include aunts, uncles, cousins, and even pets.

4 Ask your child to print "My Family Tree" at the top of the sheet. He could also name all the family members, add their birth dates, and add arrows pointing to their pictures.

My family tree

grandfather   grandmother

dad   mom   uncle   aunt

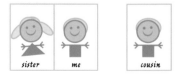

sister   me   cousin

Making a picture poem

This activity is a change from structured story writing and allows your child to discover how much fun language can be. In a picture poem, the words form the shape of the poem's subject. Almost any subject works. Here are a few examples:

Snail poem

- Ask your child to write the words of a poem following the spiral curl of a snail's shell. Encourage him to use "s" words to match the snail, like "slippery" and "slidey."

Sea poem

- Ask your child to write the words of the poem to make waves, using "w" words such as "wet" and "windy."

Moon poem

- Ask your child to write the poem to form the shape of a crescent moon, using words describing its silvery light.

Animal poem

- This could be about the movement of an animal, for example, a hopping rabbit.

Tip box ■ When your child has decided on the subject of his poem, read him other poems on that subject to give him some ideas. Then help him to write down his ideas, and to look at ways to form the words into the shape of the subject.

Reading with your child

Having completed the word-building and reading activities, your child should now be able to read three- and four-letter phonetic words, and some sight words. Your child is now ready for his first reading book. There are many books written especially for first-time readers. You will need to select a phonetic-based reading model, where the books are graded carefully, introducing new vocabulary at each level. Choose books that have some of the same nouns that your child can already read. You will find that the books will follow the same structure, and will build through words to phrases and sentences, just as in the activities in this chapter.

- Be very positive and encouraging when presenting a new book to your child. Tell him the title of the book, and discuss with him, from looking at the picture on the cover, what the story might be about.
- Explain to your child that he is going to start by looking at the pictures. By doing this first, he gets an idea of the story before attempting to read.
- Tell him that he already knows some of the words in the book. Go through the book and find the words that he is already familiar with. Encourage him to read the words; this will reassure him that he will be able to read the book.
- Go back to the beginning so that he can read the story. Put your finger under each word that he is reading, and ask him to "sound out" the phonetic sounds of the individual letters just as he did in the reading activities.
- As he gains in confidence, he will begin to recognize the words without the need to sound them out. For new sight words, you will need to read them to your child, but eventually, through

- repetition, he will begin to recognize them for himself.
- If you want to reinforce key sight words, you could make some flash cards to show him.
- Never be tempted to cover the pictures when your child is reading "to see if he really knows the words." The pictures help to decode the words.
- Spend no longer than ten minutes on each reading session. Discuss the story with your child and let him ask questions about it.
- When your child completes a book, let him know how pleased you are with his reading.
- Always review and repeat books, and do not be tempted to move on to the next book until your child is confident about reading the present book.
- Finally, remember that these books are for your child, and although you may not find their content thrilling, your child certainly will!

Numeracy skills

Montessori observed that mathematics is an abstract concept and she felt that for children to be able to understand it, she needed to make it as concrete as possible. The activities in this chapter follow this principle; they start with concrete examples, and move toward the abstract. Parents are often very surprised that children can find numbers thrilling. Children view math problems like magic spells, and they also take great comfort from the fact that $2 + 2 = 4$, and that it will always make four, in any situation. Also included are number games that will engage your child so that she will not even be aware that she is learning math.

Sorting into sets

This is a simple activity that requires sorting objects into matching sets. When your child has grasped this concept, the activity progresses to sorting objects by color, shape, and size.

You will need

- 4 sets of small objects (for example, pencils, beads, clothespins, buttons, etc.)
- Basket or container to hold objects
- 4 lengths of string, about 20 in (50 cm) each

Other activities to try

Return the objects to the basket, and ask your child to sort them by color. Start your child off with an example of each color.

Use an assortment of wooden shapes, and ask your child to sort by shape, for example, triangles, squares, and circles. (If you don't have wooden shapes, photocopy the shapes on Worksheet 2.)

1 Ask your child to take the basket to a carpeted area on the floor, and to sit next to you on your left. Put the basket in front of your child and ask him what objects are in the basket. Explain that the objects are all jumbled up and need to be sorted into sets.

2 Take your lengths of string and make circles around the outside of the basket or container. Put one of each object into each circle.

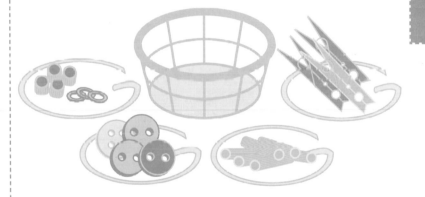

3 Ask your child to sort the rest of the objects into the circles of string.

Learning one to ten

This activity uses number rods (see page 59) to teach what the quantity of each numeral means. The "Other activities to try" section reinforces this work, by sorting with numerals, and spotting the "odd quantity out." Please note that the language changes as the activity progresses; this helps your child to further understand the concept of quantity.

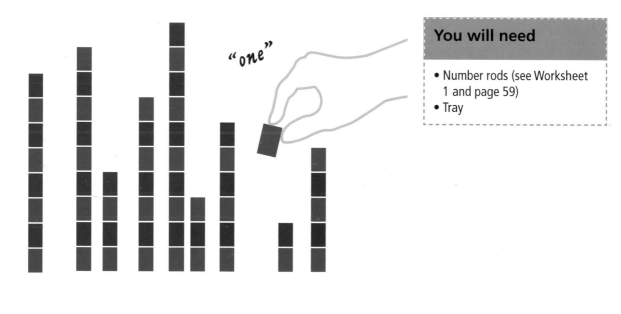

"one"

Tip box   ■ Make sure that your child always points at the numeral and says it out loud.   ■ If your child cannot remember the name of the numeral, go back to an earlier stage.

1 Put the first two number rods onto the tray and ask your child to carry the tray to the table. Ask your child to sit on your left and put the tray on your right.

2 Take rod one, and put it in front of your child. Put your index finger on it and say, "This is one." Repeat with rod two. Ask your child to repeat the numeral as you say it. Repeat twice more, using both rods.

3 Put both rods in front of your child, and say to her, "Can you point to the one?" Encourage her to put her finger on it. Repeat with two. Move the rods around, and repeat the same steps, but say, "Show me . . ." Repeat for a third time, but say, "Which is the . . .?"

4 Place both rods in front of your child, and put your finger on the one. Say, "What is this?" She should reply, "One." Now put your finger on the two and ask "What is this?" She should reply, "Two."

5 Encourage your child to count both rods, and to say, "One, two."

6 Reverse the rods and repeat the same steps twice more.

Other activities to try

Teach the quantities up to ten using the number rods. First introduce three, four, and five, then six, seven, and eight, and finally nine and ten. Each time, review the numerals from the previous session.

As your child begins to recognize number quantities, introduce counting groups of objects (you could use the sets from the previous activity). Ask, "Which set has the largest number of objects?", "Which set has the smallest number of objects?" and "Which set has a number of objects equal to another?"

Organize the objects into sets with equal numbers of objects, except for one. As your child counts each set, she will need to establish which set does not have the same number as all the other sets.

Objects on a line

This activity reinforces the concept of quantities up to ten. You need to collect lots of small objects for this activity, so I suggest you involve your child as you "count up" objects. Look for favorite objects that your child will enjoy displaying on a line across her room.

1 Put all the objects, food bags, and clothespins onto a tray, and ask your child to carry the tray to the table. Ask your child to sit on your left and put the tray in front of her.

Tip box   ■ Hang the string at a level so that your child can see the objects. Make sure that it does not become an obstruction.
■ Use large bags so that the objects fit.

2 Tell your child that she is going to make a number line, starting from one and going to ten.

3 Ask her to sort the objects into sets. Ask your child to find the set with only one object and to put it in one of the bags. Show your child how to roll over the top of the bag and seal it with the clothespin. Put the bag at the top of the table.

4 Now ask her what numeral comes after one. (If she can't remember, give her any two objects to count, and this should jog her memory.)

5 Ask her to find the set with two objects, and to put them in the bag and pin it up. Repeat the same steps for the rest of the numbers up to ten.

6 Tell your child that she is going to display the bags on a number line. Put the bags back on the tray, and ask your child to take them to the prepared line. Ask her to find the bag with one object and pass it to you so that you can hang it on the line on the left side. Repeat until all the bagged objects are on the line in a row from one to ten.

Learning numerals 1 to 10

Once your child understands the quantities one to ten, she can be taught the numerals 1 to 10. This activity uses numerals made from sandpaper, to teach the direction and shape of the numerals.

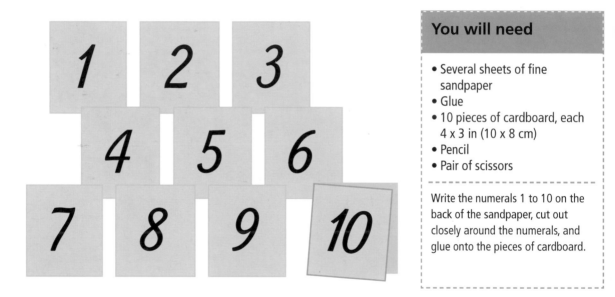

You will need

- Several sheets of fine sandpaper
- Glue
- 10 pieces of cardboard, each 4 x 3 in (10 x 8 cm)
- Pencil
- Pair of scissors

Write the numerals 1 to 10 on the back of the sandpaper, cut out closely around the numerals, and glue onto the pieces of cardboard.

1 Ask your child to take the 1 and 2 cards to the table, and to sit on your left.

2 Place card 1 in front of your child. Trace it with your index and third finger. As you are tracing, say, "This is how we write one." Let your child trace the 1, and as she does so say, "This is how we write one."

3 Repeat with card 2. Repeat with both cards twice over, but just say "one" or "two" as you, and then your child, trace the numeral.

4 Place both numerals in front of your child and say, "Show me the one" and "Show me the two." Reverse the numerals and ask, "Which is the one?" and "Which is the two?"

5 Repeat the same steps, but this time say, "Can you trace the one?" and then, "Can you trace the two?"

6 With both numerals in front of your child, point to the "1" and ask, "What is this?" When she has answered correctly, ask her to trace it. Repeat with the "2" card. Reverse the numerals and repeat the same steps.

Other activities to try

Teach the rest of the numerals up to 10, with 3, 4, and 5 first, then 6, 7, and 8, and finally, 9 and 10. Review the previous numerals before teaching new ones.

To reinforce the numerals, use a baking sheet half-filled with salt, and encourage your child to trace the numerals in the salt. You might want to print the numerals on a strip of paper that your child can refer to.

Tip box
- If your child is unable to give the name of the numeral, repeat the earlier stages.
- Encourage your child to trace the numeral as she is saying it; this makes it a visual, tactile, and auditory experience, which helps the learning process.
- Do not teach more than two or three new numerals a day.

Reinforcing the sequence of numerals

This game will help to reinforce the numerals and sequence of 1 to 10. It is also a guide to how confident your child is in these areas. In addition, your child will practice using the words "before" and "after."

You will need

- Large sheet of oak tag
- Black felt pen
- Pair of scissors
- Paper clip

Print the numerals 0 to 10 on the oak tag, allowing space to cut them into squares.

1 Ask your child to take the numeral cards to the table, and to sit on your left. Put the numerals in front of your child in a row, left to right in numerical order.

$$0\ 1\ 2\ 3\ 4\ 5\ 6\ 7\ 8\ 9\ 10$$

2 Point to a numeral and ask your child to tell you what the numeral is. Then ask him what the numeral is before and after it.

3 Repeat several times, pointing to different numerals until they have all been covered. You can also ask questions, such as, "Which is the bigger numeral, eight or ten?" or "Which is the smaller numeral, three or four?"

Other activities to try

When your child is confident with the sequence of numerals, repeat the game, but this time, turn over the numerals before and after, so your child cannot use them as reference. When he guesses, turn them over to show him whether he is correct.

Put the numerals in a row left to right, in order. Remove three of the numerals and turn them face down. Ask your child to turn over one of the numerals and find where it should go in the sequence. Repeat with the other two numerals. As your child gains more confidence, remove more numerals out of the sequence.

Combining quantities and numerals

This activity combines your child's understanding of quantity, using the numerals 1 to 10. Before your child attempts this activity, review the activity "Learning height and length" on pages 58–59.

You will need

- Number cards from previous activity (see page 114)
- Number rods (Worksheet 1, and see pages 58–59)
- Tray

Tip box ■ Take this opportunity to introduce other ways of asking for a numeral. This helps with language and mathematical skills. For example, use, "Find the . . ." or "What is this . . .?"

1 Put the cards and rods onto the tray and ask your child to carry it to the table. Place the number rods horizontally in front of your child in any order. Place the number cards to the right in any order.

Other activities to try

When you see that your child can match the rods and cards, show her how to build the rods and cards into numerical order. Start with the rods, and build the staircase, as in the activity on pages 58–59. When this is complete, show your child how to match the cards with the rods, showing 1 and 2 only. Invite your child to complete the matching.

2 Ask your child, "Can you find the four rod?" Your child will need to count the rods until she finds the correct rod.

3 Now say, "Can you find how we print four?" When your child finds the "4" card, ask her to place it at the end of the four rod.

4 Choose another numeral, and follow the same steps. Continue until all the number cards have been placed next to their matching quantity (rod).

Cups and counters

This is another activity to reinforce the numerals with their corresponding quantity. This activity also introduces the concept of zero (0).

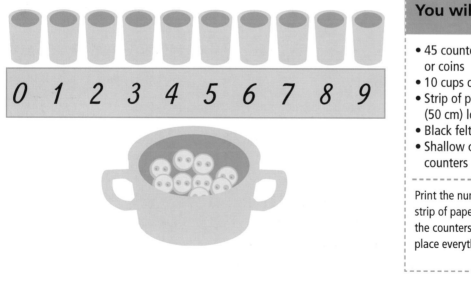

You will need

- 45 counters, buttons, beads, or coins
- 10 cups or small containers
- Strip of paper about 20 in (50 cm) long
- Black felt pen
- Shallow container to hold counters

Print the numerals 0 to 9 across the strip of paper, spaced evenly. Put the counters into the container and place everything onto a tray.

Tip box ■ The activity uses 45 counters, which is exactly what your child will need to be able to count up to nine. If she has too few or too many at the end, it will be a clue to check the cups.
■ Make sure you start with the correct amount!

Other activity to try

Return to the "Counting objects" activity on pages 110–111. Take another bag to match the others, and place it before the "1" bag on the line. Explain to your child that it represents zero. Ask her if she can remember what zero means. She should reply "nothing." Then ask her if she will need to put anything in the bag. If she has any difficulty remembering, you can give her hints, such as reminding her that it comes before one.

1 Ask your child to carry the tray to the table and to sit on your left. Place the container with the counters in front of her and the number strip behind, and place the cups in a row behind the paper strip.

2 Point to the number strip and ask your child to read the numerals on it. Return to the "0" and say that it is called "zero." Explain that it means "nothing," so she will be putting no counters in that cup.

3 Point to the "1" and ask your child to put that number of counters in the cup above.

4 Point to the "2" and repeat the same instructions. Repeat for "3" and "4." Continue to "9" if your child would like to.

5 If you notice that she has put an incorrect number of counters into a cup, do not be tempted to correct her at this point. When she has completed the activity, say, "Let's check that we have the right number of counters in the cups." When you are counting together, allow her to discover that she has made an error in her counting.

Numbers out of sequence

This activity reinforces counting and matching the correct quantity to the relevant numeral. However, there is a further move from the concrete to the abstract as now the numerals are loose, and not written in order. This activity also introduces the concept of "odd" and "even" numbers.

1 Ask your child to take the container with the counters to the table. You take the number cards. Ask your child to sit on your left with the containers in front of her. Mix the cards, and place them above the container to your child's right.

2 Ask your child to find the numeral one, and to place the card on her left above the container. Then ask how many counters she will need to place under it. Ask her to place the counter under the numeral.

3 Ask your child what comes after one. Encourage her to find the number "2" card, and then two counters to place underneath, side by side.

4 Follow the steps for numerals "3" or "4," then ask your child to continue to number ten by herself. Give her some guidance on the placement of the counters; the "even" number counters need to be in two columns next to each other, while the "odd" number counters need to have the extra counter placed on the left-hand column.

5 If your child makes a mistake with the sequence of numerals, wait until she has completed the activity, then ask her to compare her numerals with the number strip used for the previous activity.

Other activities to try

When your child can work independently at this activity, point to the counters and ask if she notices any similarity about them. Explain that numbers that can be put into pairs, such as 2, 4, and 6 are known as "even" numbers. Also explain that numbers without a pair, such as 1, 3, and 5 are known as "odd" numbers.

To reinforce odd and even numbers, set out four small objects in the same pattern as the counters. Ask your child to count the objects. Ask if the three or four is an odd or even number. If she is not sure, remind her about the rule of even numbers always having a "partner," while odd numbers always have one left over.

When you are out with your child, point out how house numbers are in order on opposite sides of the street in odd and even numbers (use a street that starts from 1).

Teach your child that all "odd" numbers have 1, 3, 5, 7, and 9 in them, while all "even" numbers have 0, 2, 4, 6, and 8 in them. Show your child some examples in your home or local area.

Adding numerals to objects

Now that your child has learned both the quantities and numerals from 0 to 10, you can add the numerals to the "Objects on a line" already created (see pages 110–111).

You will need

- Number cards from previous activities (see pages 114–115)
- Black felt pen
- Colored pens or pencils

Draw around each numeral using the pen, to create large numerals with space for your child to color in.

Other activity to try

Make cardboard ladybugs without their spots. Involve your child in coloring the ladybug, and work with her to add the spots, from 0 to 10. When complete, hang them on the line across the room. This is a time-consuming and enjoyable activity, so you might want to spread it over a week.

1 Ask your child to color in the numerals. When she has finished, explain to her that the numerals are going to be put up on the "Objects on a line" you made before.

2 Lay out the number cards under the object number line in a random order. Point to the first bag and ask your child if there is anything in the bag. She should respond with "no." You respond with "Which numeral is the same as nothing?" Point to the numerals on the floor and she should pick out the "0." Help her to pin it to the empty bag.

3 Point to the bag with one object in it, and ask her, "How many objects are in this bag?" Ask her to find the number "1," and help her to add it to the line. Continue these steps until you reach "10."

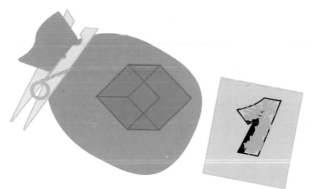

Tip box ■ If your child can't remember the next number quantity, take the bag off the line and ask her to count the objects.

Addition up to 10

Now that your child has learned the quantities and numerals from 0 to 10, you can introduce her to addition. This activity follows the same pattern as the other number activities, so that it begins adding quantity, and only later introduces the numerals and signs required.

You will need

- Number rods (Worksheet 1, and see pages 58–59)
- Tray

1 Ask your child to carry the tray with the number rods to the table. Put the number rods in a random order in front of her. Ask her to build the number rods into a stair (see pages 58–59).

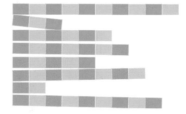

2 Say, "I am going to show you how to do addition using the number rods." Ask your child to find the

1 rod, and to place it below the stair. Then ask her to find a number rod, for example, 4, and to put it next to the 1. Select numbers under five, to keep it easy.

3 Ask her to count along the joined rods to see what number she gets. Make sure that your child uses a finger to count carefully each number rod section. When she gives the answer, "five," explain that "1 plus 4 equals 5." As you are saying this, point to the individual number rods.

4 Ask your child to put back the rods, and then do several more addition problems, remembering to use low numbers.

5 When your child understands the objective of the activity, tell her that she can make up her own problem. Ask her to choose two numbers, then ask her to tell you the answer, for example, "5 plus 3 equals . . ." You may need to explain the words "plus" and "equals" to her.

6 When she has finished the activity, review the steps that got her to her answer. Remind her that the number she finishes with must always be bigger than the two numbers she started with.

Addition using numerals

When your child has mastered the concept of addition with quantities (using number rods), introduce numerals. This activity uses the number cards used in previous activities to construct a problem. As your child progresses, introduce problems written on paper (see "Other activity to try").

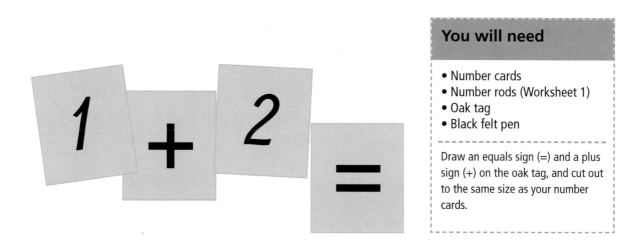

You will need

- Number cards
- Number rods (Worksheet 1)
- Oak tag
- Black felt pen

Draw an equals sign (=) and a plus sign (+) on the oak tag, and cut out to the same size as your number cards.

1 Lay out the number cards and number rods in order. Ask your child to choose a number rod and to place it on the table in front of her.

2 Ask your child to find the matching number card, and to place it under the number rod. Place the "+" card next to the selected number card, and explain that it means "plus."

3 Ask your child to select another number rod, and to place it after the plus sign. Place the "=" card after the second number, and explain that it is the sign for "equals."

4 Ask your child what she needs to do next, and she should tell you, "Count the numbers" or "Add them together." Help her to find the answer, using the number rods to count, if necessary.

5 When she finds the answer, put it next to the equals sign. Do several more problems with your child until she is ready to make up her own problems.

Other activity to try

When your child is confident with the number cards, introduce working problems written on paper. She may also eventually like to make up her own problems.

Subtraction under 10

Generally, children find the concept of subtraction easier to grasp than addition. For example, they often understand that if you have six apples, and give three away, that there are three apples left. You might like to try this activity before the previous one.

Because your child will already be familiar with doing addition problems, both the quantity and the numerals are introduced at the same time in this activity.

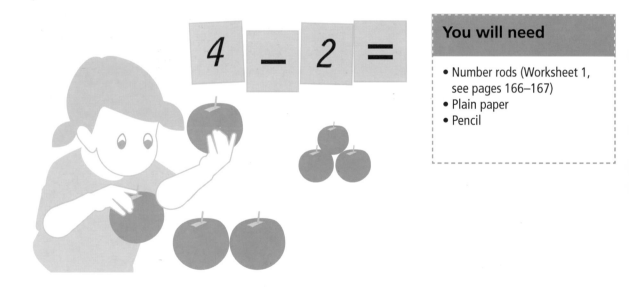

You will need

- Number rods (Worksheet 1, see pages 166–167)
- Plain paper
- Pencil

1 Ask your child to take the number rods to the table and to sit on your left. Ask her to build the number rods into a stair, leaving a space below.

2 Take out two rods and place them together. Ask your child to count the sections and find the total. Remove the lowest number rod, and ask your child to count what is left. Do two more problems in this way, so that your child begins to see the processes involved.

3 When the fourth problem has been completed, repeat the steps but add questions such as, "We started with how many?" and "Then we took away how many?" and "We were left with how many?" Finish by summarizing, for example, "So 5 take away 3 leaves 2."

4 Show your child how to write the problem on paper, explaining that this is how we write this problem. Do two more problems in this way, with you doing the writing for your child.

5 When your child is ready to do the problem, ask her to do it as she goes through the steps. Otherwise, she will forget the number that she started with, and the number she "took away."

Other activities to try

Write a minus (–) sign on a card and use the number cards from the previous activity to work through more problems.

When your child is confident with the number cards, introduce working problems written on paper.

Show your child addition and subtraction in everyday situations. For example, demonstrate with fruit, blocks, toys, etc.

Introducing money

As a child I used to love "playing store" and the children that I teach still love this activity. It gives them a realistic experience of addition and subtraction, as well as being a good introduction to the concept of money.

Other activities to try

As well as food, include household items like soap, laundry detergent, toothpaste, shampoo, etc.

Set up a clothing, shoe-, or bookstore. You could also try a post office, with stamps, letters, and packages to send.

This activity is ideal for when your child has friends around; it will keep them occupied for a long time.

1 Assemble a store using the equipment listed, and involve your children. Ask who would like to name the store. Write prices on the packages or on pieces of cardboard that you prop against the foods. Choose prices that are less than 10 cents. Put each coin type into a separate container and ask your child to sort the rest. Finally, ask your child to make an "Open" and "Closed" sign to be turned over when needed.

2 Decide who is to be the shopkeeper and who is to be the customer. Give the customer some money and the shopping basket.

3 Play at buying foods, using a simple exchange, with an item being bought for the exact money.

4 When your children are familiar with this, introduce simple addition. Use the exact money, with no change.

5 Finally, when they have mastered this, introduce subtraction with a purchase that requires change.

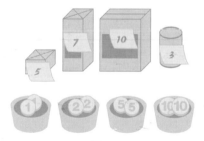

Tip box ■ This activity affords an excellent opportunity for extending language skills, so have some fun with it. If you are the shopkeeper, mention any special offers you may have today, say hello and good-bye, and encourage your customer to buy a new product. If you are the customer, comment on how nice the store looks, what tasty-looking foods are on display, etc.

Number songs and rhymes

These are an excellent way to reinforce numbers and numerical concepts because of the rhyming element and the actions, which act as a memory aid. They can be taught to children of any age.

Once I Caught A Fish Alive

This song reinforces the numerical sequence, and counting in ones. Count out the numbers on your fingers as you say them.

One, two, three, four, five,
Once I caught a fish alive.
Six, seven, eight, nine, ten;
Then I let him go again.
Why did you let him go?
Because he bit my finger so.
Which finger did he bite?
This little finger on my right.

One, Two, Buckle My Shoe

This song also counts in numerical order. You could count out the numbers on your fingers, and do some of the actions.

One, two, buckle my shoe,
Three, four, knock at the door,
Five, six, pick up sticks,
Seven, eight, lay them straight,
Nine, ten, a big fat hen.

Ten Fat Sausages

This song is a firm favorite with the children I teach. It also involves subtraction, and counting down in twos. When you get to "pop," make a pop sound with your index finger inside your mouth. Clap your hands together for "bang."

Ten fat sausages sizzling in a pan,
One went pop and the other went bang.
Eight fat sausages sizzling in a pan,
One went pop and the other went bang.
Six fat sausages sizzling in a pan, etc.

Ten Currant Buns

Children really enjoy acting out this song with someone being the baker and another person coming to buy the buns. You could also have real buns or cookies and some pennies.

Ten currant buns in a baker's shop
Round and fat with a cherry on the top.
Along came [your child's name]
With a penny one day,
[He/she] bought a currant bun
And took it right away.
Nine currant buns, etc.

Ten Green Bottles

You could use plastic bottles to follow the actions, or you could change the words to use teddy bears or other suitable objects.

Ten green bottles hanging on a wall,
Ten green bottles hanging on a wall,
And if one green bottle should accidentally fall,
There'll be nine green bottles hanging on the wall.

Science skills

In Montessori, we teach science in the broadest
sense of the word, covering everything from
botany to geography, and the activities in this
chapter cover this wide spectrum. Children find
the world around them an endless source of
interest, and this is reflected in questions of
"Why?" "I wonder?" and "What if?"

The activities on the following pages will
engage your child's imagination and set him on
a voyage of discovery that has many pathways.
Rather than being given immediate answers to his
questions, he will learn to observe and wait, as
well as to understand the processes involved. This
increases a sense of wonderment, and gives your
child a deeper understanding of the world around
him. It also increases self-esteem, because he will
learn to find out the answers to his own questions.

Collecting leaves

Children are a little bit like squirrels in their hoarding habits. They enjoy finding "treasures" in the backyard, and then hiding them away. This next activity harnesses this enthusiasm and at the same time teaches that natural things fall into "family" groups, each with its own name.

You will need

- Sheets of white paper
- Wax crayons, preferably in leaf colors

1 When out with your child in the park or backyard, suggest that he collect some leaves. Suggest different shapes, for example, "Can you find me a star-shaped leaf?" or "Can you find me a thin, narrow leaf?" This way you should get a good variety of leaves. Try to collect four to six varieties, and several of each.

2 Put the leaves into a suitable container. Put one leaf from each family in a row on the table, and ask your child to sort the rest.

3 Take a sheet of white paper and place one of the leaves under it. Take a crayon and rub it over the paper to reveal the leaf and its details. Have the crayon on its side for best results.

4 Let your child choose another leaf so that he can try. You may need to help hold the paper still while he does the rubbing.

Other activities to try

Your child could examine the leaves under a magnifying glass, to see the veins.

You may want to help your child make a display of the leaf rubbings by making an autumn scene. Draw a tree or trees on a large piece of paper. Ask your child to cut out the crayoned leaves and stick them onto the branches. You may want to include other things like nuts or mushrooms, or drawings of some forest animals.

When outside, collect acorns in autumn, and flowers in spring. You could use these to make artwork and displays, and to tell your child about the seasons.

Tip box ■ Children find the rubbing action quite tricky, as it requires a certain amount of pressure with a strong outward pushing motion. You might need to help, and provide thick, good-quality paper.

Make a flower puzzle

This activity serves a double purpose in that while your child is making and constructing a puzzle of a flower, he is learning about the parts of a flower and the names of those parts.

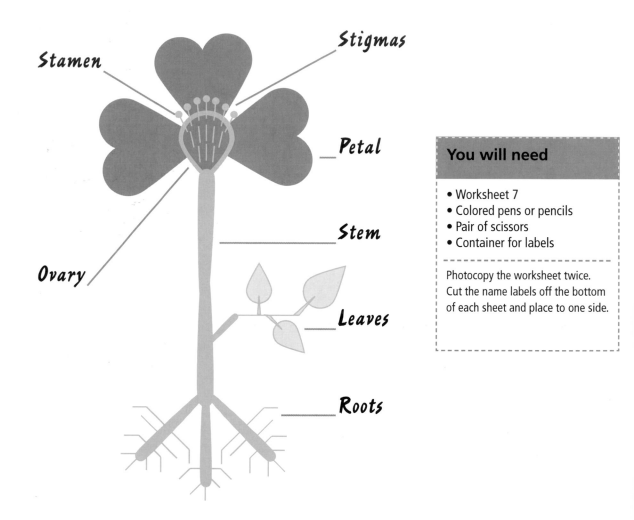

Stamen

Stigmas

Petal

Stem

Ovary

Leaves

Roots

You will need

- Worksheet 7
- Colored pens or pencils
- Pair of scissors
- Container for labels

Photocopy the worksheet twice. Cut the name labels off the bottom of each sheet and place to one side.

1 Take the photocopies and ask your child to shade in the flowers. When he has finished, tell him that you are going to show him how to make a puzzle.

2 Cut one flower picture into six to eight pieces, trying to keep the petals and other parts intact.

3 Place the uncut flower in front of your child, as a guide for building the puzzle. Ask him to put the pieces together to make the puzzle.

4 As soon as your child can construct the puzzle independently, remove the guide flower and use it only if needed for reference.

Growing carrot tops

In this activity children can learn about the regenerative nature of plants and how shoots can emerge from an already fully grown carrot. It takes only a few days for new leaves to sprout.

You will need

- 2 carrots with green leaves or shoots on top
- 2 saucers
- Pitcher of water

Trim the carrots so there are just a few leaves or shoots on top. Cut off the main part of the carrots, so you have about ¾ in (2 cm) left.

1 Put all the items on a tray and carry them to the table. Ask your child, "Do you think we can make these carrots start growing again?" Whatever answer you get, say, "Let's see what happens."

2 Put the carrot tops on each saucer and pass them to your child. Now ask your child, "What do you think these carrot tops will need to help them to grow?" You may need to give some hints like, "What do we need when we get thirsty?" When he gives the answer of water, pass over the water pitcher and ask him to pour a little water in each saucer.

3 Tell your child that he needs to watch the carrot tops for the next few days and see what happens. Ask him to check that there is enough water in the saucers. The carrots should sprout new leaves on top.

Growing broad beans

This is an excellent activity for observing all the stages of plant growth; even the root stage is visible through the glass jar.

1 Show your child the bean seeds, the paper towels and sand, and explain that this is what you are going to use to grow bean seeds. Ask him to put the sand into the jars.

2 Fold enough paper towels over double to fit around the inside of one jar and ask your child to put it in the jar on top of the sand. Hand him one of the bean seeds and ask him to slide it down the jar between the paper and glass a little above the sand.

3 Repeat the same steps for the other bean seed. Ask your child what he thinks needs to be added to the seeds to help make them grow. If he is not sure, remind him about the carrot-growing experiment.

4 Ask him to add water by drizzling it with his fingertips over the paper. Explain that he will need to check to see that the paper does not dry out, and to add more water if necessary. Ask him to observe which part of the plant appears first.

You will need

- 3 glass jars or glasses
- Paper towels
- Sand to quarter-fill each jar or glass
- Pitcher of water
- 3 broad bean seeds

Other activities to try

Show your child how to make a diary by sketching the different growing stages of the bean plants.

When you are in the backyard or park with your child, examine all the different types of plants, their structure and leaf size, and talk about why some plants have thorns or prickles. You might want to take a magnifying glass with you so that your child can get a closer look. This would also be a good opportunity to look at plants that have berries and explain that the berries are strictly for the birds.

Growing sunflowers

If ever there was a flower with a "wow" factor for a child, then the sunflower is it. It starts as a tiny seed and grows to a tall height, all in the space of one season. Check which variety of sunflower you buy; go for the tallest possible.

You will need

- Giant sunflower seeds
- Picture of a grown sunflower
- 3 to 5 small potting pots and saucers
- Potting compost for each pot
- Pitcher of water
- Tray

1 Put the pots, seeds, compost, and pitcher of water on the tray.

2 Tell your child that she is going to plant some sunflower seeds. Show her the seeds and then show her a picture of a sunflower. Tell her that when fully grown, the sunflower might be taller than mommy or daddy.

3 Ask your child to fill each pot with about 1 in (2.5 cm) of compost and then tell her to put a seed in each pot. Then ask her to put in the rest of the compost up to 1½ in (4 cm) from the top, and to water each pot.

4 Find a sunny spot for the pots, and ask your child to check the soil daily to see if it needs any water. As the sunflowers grow, you will need to support them with a stick, and eventually plant them out in the garden or in a larger pot.

Other activities to try

Growing sunflowers provides an excellent opportunity for introducing measuring. Instead of a ruler, your child can use her hands, with the heel of the palm to the fingertips. Record the measurements along with the date.

When the sunflowers are taller than your child, record this with a photograph, and as they continue to grow, take more photographs of other family members, so that your child has a visual comparison.

Planting a window box

This activity can be done whatever the size of your home. Your child can be involved in the whole process and, at the same time, learn something about the cyclical nature of plants by planting them, watching them develop, and finally, seeing the herbs used.

Take your child to a garden center and let him help to choose a selection of herbs for the window box. Show him the different pictures of the plants so he will know what they will look like when they are flowering.

You will need

- Window box or pot
- Herb plants
- Compost
- Drainage material (for example, broken flower pots)
- Newspaper

Other activities to try

If possible, pick fruits, herbs, and vegetables from the garden with your child, and show him that you are using them in cooking.

Visit a farmstand or a pick-your-own place to buy fresh produce that you later use at home.

1 This activity is best done on a table outside. If this is not possible, protect your kitchen table with old newspaper.

2 Place the herb pots and planting equipment on the table and tell your child that he is going to plant a window box that will flower in the spring. Start by putting a handful of drainage material into the bottom of the box, and invite him to do the rest. Add the compost so that it reaches about a quarter full.

3 Select one of the plants and show your child how it is planted into the compost. Let him plant the rest of the herbs and then show him how to add compost until it reaches a few inches from the rim.

4 Move the box to its growing position, preferably a sheltered, ground-level windowsill where your child will be able to observe as the plants develop. Now ask him to check the soil every week, to see if it needs watering.

How plants drink water

With the aid of food coloring, your child will be able to track the course of the water taken in by a flower, until it reaches the flower head. In the extension activity, he will be able to cut open celery to see how the water has traveled through the vegetable's capillaries.

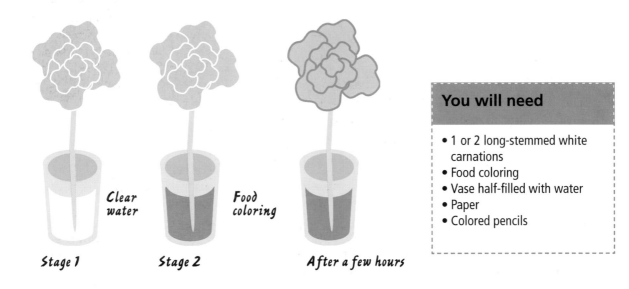

Clear water

Stage 1

Food coloring

Stage 2

After a few hours

You will need

- 1 or 2 long-stemmed white carnations
- Food coloring
- Vase half-filled with water
- Paper
- Colored pencils

1 Place the vase containing the carnations in front of your child. On the sheet of paper, ask him to draw a picture of the vase containing the flowers on the left side of the sheet (he will need to make two other drawings).

2 Ask him to add a few drops of food coloring to the water in the vase and use a teaspoon to stir the water in the vase until the color is evenly distributed.

3 Now ask him to make a second drawing next to the first, and to color in the water. Leave the flowers for a few hours.

4 When you return to the flowers, your child should observe that the flower heads are no longer white but have changed to the color of the colored water. Ask him what he thinks may have happened. To help him understand, you can ask him to think about what happens when he has a drink through a straw, and tell him that the stem of the flower is like the straw.

5 Finally, ask him to draw the colored flower heads. He may also want to number the drawings and give further explanation by adding words like "food coloring."

Other activity to try

Repeat the activity, using a stalk of celery. Chop off one end, so it will absorb the water. When you return to the celery, cut it into several sections. Your child will discover that the food coloring has traveled up the stem of the celery. He may also notice that the color at the top of the stem is not as strong as at the bottom. Explain that the water has traveled up through tiny tubes called capillaries.

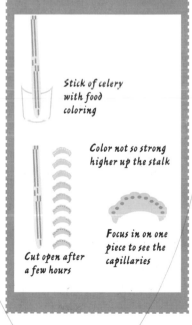

Stick of celery with food coloring

Color not so strong higher up the stalk

Cut open after a few hours

Focus in on one piece to see the capillaries

Understanding volume

This is a simple and effective introduction to volume and its estimation. In the first activity, two containers are chosen and your child will need to estimate which container holds more water. The choice of containers is very important; one should be tall and thin – for example, a small vase – while the other should be shorter and wider – for example, a water glass. The latter should hold the greater volume of water. The aim of the activity is that your child will come to understand that height is not the only thing to be considered when estimating volume.

You will need

- Tall vase
- A glass that is shorter and wider than the vase, and holds more water
- Funnel
- Liquid measuring cup

1. Put the two containers in front of your child. Ask your child which container he thinks holds the most water and then tell him that he is going to find out by measuring.

2. Ask him to fill the vase up with water using the measuring cup, and then pour it into the glass with the aid of the funnel. Draw his attention to the level of water in the glass.

3. Now ask your child to fill up the vase with water from the glass. When the vase is almost full, stop him from pouring any more water in. Draw his attention to the fact that there is still water in the glass. Ask him if there was any water left in the vase when it was poured into the glass. From this, he will be able to draw the conclusion that the shorter, wider glass holds the most water.

4. If you want to do a double check, you could show your child how to measure the amount of water in each container using the measuring cup.

Other activity to try

Set out an assortment of containers in a row in front of your child, and put a small cup in front. Tell him that he needs to try and guess how many cups of water each container holds. Going along the row, ask him to first estimate, and then count out the number of cups each container actually holds. Get him to record each answer on a piece of paper by drawing a picture of the container and then writing the estimate and then the actual measure of cups next to it. If when measuring out the water it looks like it may overflow, stop, and show him how to record it as a half.

Floating and sinking objects

Before your child carries out this experiment, the next time he takes
a bath, draw his attention to the fact that some of his bath toys
always float, and yet the soap sinks to the bottom of the bath.
Tell him that he can investigate this further the next day.

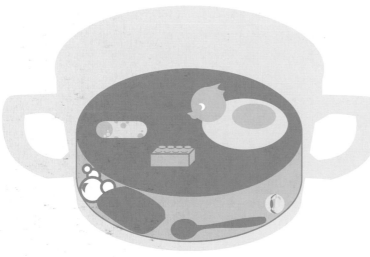

You will need

- An assortment of small
  objects, some that float and
  some that sink, such as a
  teaspoon, cup, bath toy, cork,
  and sponge
- Large bowl half-filled with
  water
- Paper
- Pencil

There may be some splashing,
so protect the tabletop. Put all the
small objects onto a tray. On the
sheet of paper, draw an outline of
the side of the bowl with a line to
mark the water level.

1 Put all the objects in a row in front of your child, with the bowl of water behind them. Say that he is going to find out which objects float and which sink.

2 Pick up the first object in the row and say whether you think it will float or sink. Drop it into the water gently. Invite your child to estimate, and then test the rest of the objects, to see whether they float or sink.

3 Help your child to record what happens by drawing the objects on the picture of the bowl. Show the objects above and below the waterline as they sink or float.

Other activities to try

After he has recorded his findings, discuss with him what the objects are made from. Encourage him to conclude that certain materials are better at floating than others.

If you are using a sponge, your child should see that the sponge will float at first, but as it becomes heavier with water, it will sink.

Repeat the same experiment, but add salt to the water to see how this affects the floatability of the objects.

Take your child to look at boats and see what they are made from. Introduce him to the word "fiberglass"; explain what kind of material it is. Ask him questions such as, "Why are boats made out of fiberglass?" If he is not sure, remind him about the floating and sinking experiment. Also, point out the shape, and explain how it helps the boats to float.

Floating liquids

This is a wonderful visual experiment to show your child how liquids have different densities. Children find this experiment fascinating because the liquids form a layer in the jar according to their density.

You will need

- 1 tall clear jar, glass, or pitcher
- Corn syrup
- Glycerine
- Water colored blue with food coloring
- Sunflower oil
- Olive oil
- Metal tablespoon
- Paper
- Colored pencil
- Tray

1 Transfer some of each liquid into pitchers or containers so that your child can pour it into the larger vessel. Make a drawing of the jar, glass, or pitcher on the sheet of paper, then put all the materials on the tray.

2 Put the liquids in a row in front of your child with the jar, glass, or pitcher behind them. Go through the liquids, discussing with him what each liquid is. Tell your child that he is going to pour the liquids into the jar in order of their weight or density.

3 Ask your child to pour the syrup into the jar until it is a fifth full (you could mark the jar). Ask him to add the glycerine, trickling it onto the back of the tablespoon. Wait for it to settle.

4 Now ask him to add the water. Then add the sunflower oil, pouring over the spoon, and finally, the olive oil.

5 After all the liquids have been poured, ask him to draw the outcome on the sheet of paper. After the liquids have been drawn, your child or you could write the names of the liquids alongside.

Other activity to try

Take each of the liquids listed above and put each in a jar to the same level. Ask your child to drop a marble into one jar and to count out loud as the marble sinks to the bottom. Repeat with the other liquids. Ask your child why he thinks it took the marble longer to reach the bottom of the jar with some of the liquids. This will introduce him to the concept of density.

Discovering the weather

In this next activity, your child can investigate how a pinecone is sensitive to changes in weather. This investigation is just one example of how plants and animals are able to "read" changes in weather patterns, and there are others to investigate in the extension activities. You might want to plan this activity for a day when rain is due.

You will need

• A closed pinecone

1 Ask your child to place the pinecone outside in a place sheltered from the sun and rain. Leave it in this place until there has been rain and the air is wet. Ask him to observe how the pinecone segments are tightly closed.

2 Ask your child to bring the pinecone into a warm room and to observe if there are any changes over the next few hours or days. The segments of the pinecone should open up in the dry air.

3 Ask your child why he thinks this change may have occurred. If he is not sure, draw his attention to the different weather conditions of wet and dry. Explain that the pinecone is "protecting" itself from the wet air. You can explain that it is similar to when your child puts on a raincoat to protect himself from the rain.

Other activities to try

When you are out in the backyard or the park, examine other plants to see if there are any changes in them between wet and dry weather. For example, flowers that close at night for protection against the dew, or sun-sensitive plants whose flowers open only in the sunlight.

Look at animals like ducks that are waterproofed against the weather, and discuss why with your child.

Encourage your child to observe different shaped clouds, and how different shaped and colored clouds bring rain.

Introducing a globe and map

What could be more abstract for a child than a map, with solid land forms being represented in two- and three-dimensional forms? The activities in this section endeavour to make that leap of understanding by making his first experience of geography as concrete as possible.

Your child will learn to familiarize himself with the globe and world map and come to understand that they both represent our planet, and he will learn that land masses are made up of continents, each with their own names.

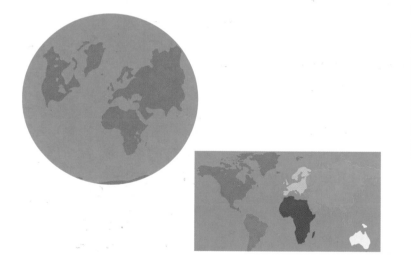

You will need

- Globe
- World map, preferably one with each continent shown in a separate color

Tip box ■ As you introduce new countries and continents, review familiar destinations first.

1 Show your child the globe and invite him to feel around it, and ask him what shape it reminds him of. He may say a ball, and you can explain that this shape is called a sphere. He may remember this from earlier activities.

2 Explain that the sphere represents planet Earth, the planet that we live on. Later on, explain that it is also called a globe. Explain that the blue represents the oceans, and the colored shapes the land.

3 Show him the country where he lives. Mention your hometown or city, and then explain that it is within a much larger country. Using your finger, trace around the outline of the country, and ask him to do the same. As he is doing this, say the name of your country.

4 Now find other destinations that he will be familiar with, such as where other family members live or where you have been on vacation. Over the next few days, introduce your child to the rest of the continents.

Other activities to try

Show him a world map, and say that it is as if we had peeled off the skin of the globe, like an orange, and laid it flat on the table. Ask your child to find your country on the globe, then ask him to find it on the map. If he is having difficulty, give him some clues, such as telling him the color of the continent. Now repeat these steps, asking him to find the other countries he may have visited.

If your child loves cars, boats, and planes, then look at the map and talk about what type of transportation you could take to reach a destination. To help him understand the concept of distance, talk about it in the terms of how many nights' sleep it would take to reach that destination.

If your child loves animals, talk about and collect pictures of the different animals to be found on the continents, and the habitat of each animal, for example, rain forest or desert. Stick the pictures of the animals onto the continents.

When you bring food home from the supermarket, show your child the label that indicates the country of origin. When the food has been eaten, save the label and stick it onto the world map. You could also ask your child to draw different fruits and to stick them on the country they are grown in. At the same time, mention the climate that these fruits grow in.

Making land models

In this activity, your child is going to make models of landforms, such as an island, lake, peninsula, bay, isthmus, and strait. By presenting these geographical landforms through the use of models, he will be able to understand the concept of these landforms in a clear, concrete way.

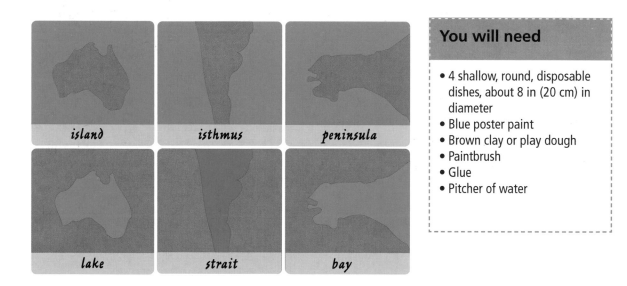

island

isthmus

peninsula

lake

strait

bay

You will need

- 4 shallow, round, disposable dishes, about 8 in (20 cm) in diameter
- Blue poster paint
- Brown clay or play dough
- Paintbrush
- Glue
- Pitcher of water

1 Ask your child to paint the inside bottom of the dishes with the blue paint.

2 When the paint is dry, ask him to make the clay into a flat shape. Stick the shape into the center of one dish, and tell him that he has made a model of an island. Say, "An island is a piece of land surrounded by water." As you are saying this, point to the land, and then the blue water. If you have used clay and waterproof paint, get him to pour in some water to surround the island.

3 Give your child some more clay, and ask him to put it around the edge of a dish to make a lake. Say, "A lake is a body of water surrounded by land." Point to the water and then the land as you are saying this, and if possible, get him to pour in some water.

Other activities to try

Follow the same steps to make more landforms, including a peninsula (a piece of land surrounded on three sides by water), a bay (a body of water surrounded on three sides by land), an isthmus (a strip of land surrounded on two sides by water), and a strait (a strip of water surrounded on two sides by land).

Help your child to find examples of these landforms on the globe and world map.

Write out the different definitions of the landforms on individual strips of paper, highlighting the name of the landform in a different color.

Mixing colors

As discussed in chapter two, color plays a very important part in your child's world and helps to shape his ideas. This next activity will reveal to your child something about the science of colors and their makeup. We begin with the three primary colors, and mix them to create the secondary colors. In the extension activity, there is more color mixing, but this time using colored inks and paper towels.

You will need

- 10 paper plates, about 10 in (25 cm) in diameter
- Red, yellow, and blue poster paint
- 3 thick paintbrushes
- Black felt pen
- Small piece of black felt or paper

Cover your working surface with old newspaper and decant the paints if necessary. Put the paper plates on the table. Use the pen to mark the base of one plate into thirds.

1 Show your child the three colors of red, yellow, and blue, and ask him to paint each third of the plate in a different color. Tell him that from these three colors, he is going to make different colors.

2 Ask your child to paint the base of one plate blue, and another plate red. Take another plate, and ask him to add some blue paint while you add a small amount of red. Ask him to mix the two colors together, and ask him what color he has made.

3 Repeat with the yellow and red paint, and ask your child what color he has made by mixing yellow and red together.

4 Repeat with the yellow and blue paint, and ask your child what color he has made by mixing yellow and blue together.

5 Review the colors beginning with the three primary colors on the first plate.

6 Make three plus signs, and three equals signs out of the black felt or paper. Display the plates on a wall like math problems, for example, blue + red = purple.

Other activity to try

Use red, yellow, and blue colored inks or food coloring and mix colors on blotting paper. Ask your child to wet a sponge and to stroke it over the paper. Ask him to squeeze a few drops of red ink onto the paper. Repeat with the blue ink, and show him how to press the two together. The colors will run together to create purple. Follow the same steps to mix other colors. This type of color blending lends itself to art activities, such as making butterflies.

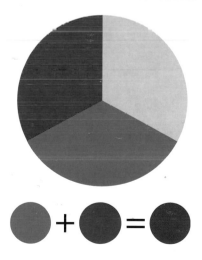

Baking fruit muffins

Cooking and baking are wonderful ways to introduce science, as they take raw materials to make something new. These activities teach practical skills, introduce new sensory experiences and vocabulary, and reinforce mathematics with weights and measures.

These muffins are the perfect size for children, and this recipe will make about 20. I have added two fruits, but you can add any fruits or flavors you prefer to the basic muffin mixture. The muffins are best baked in paper muffin cups.

You will need

- 1¼ cups all-purpose flour
- ½ tablespoon baking powder
- ¼ teaspoon of salt
- 1 egg
- 2½ tablespoons superfine sugar
- ½ cup milk
- ½ stick butter, melted and cooled slightly
- ½ teaspoon pure vanilla extract
- ½ cup small blueberries or fresh apricots, chopped
- Muffin tin or baking sheet
- Paper muffin cases

1 Preheat the oven to 400°F (200°C). Show your child how to sift the flour, baking powder, and salt into a large bowl.

2 In a separate bowl, ask her to mix together the egg, sugar, milk, melted butter, and vanilla extract. Now ask her to resift the dry ingredients into the egg mixture.

3 Fold this mixture together. I suggest you do this, as it requires gentle folding, rather than stirring or beating, to keep the muffins light.

4 Ask your child to add the fruit while you fold it in.

5 Ask your child to place paper muffin cups into the muffin tin or on the baking sheet. Give her a teaspoon, and show her how to spoon the mixture into each cup.

6 Transfer the pan to the oven, and bake for 20 minutes until the muffins are well risen and brown. Remove from the oven and transfer to a wire rack to cool. If you have not used paper cups, let them cool for 5 minutes before removing the muffins from the tin.

Making gingerbread

Children love to make gingerbread people. Not only do they get the chance to use the rolling pin, but they can let their imaginations run wild when it comes to decorating the shapes. You can also change the gingerbread figures to make different shapes for the festive season. The amount of shapes you can make will be determined by the size of your cutters.

You will need

- ¼ stick butter or margarine, plus extra for greasing
- ¼ cup brown sugar
- 2 tablespoons corn syrup
- 1 cup all-purpose flour, plus extra for dusting
- ½ teaspoon baking powder
- ½ teaspoon ground ginger
- ½ teaspoon ground cinnamon
- 1 tablespoon milk
- Gingerbread cookie cutter
- Baking sheet

For the frosting
- 1 cup confectioners' sugar
- 1 tablespoon warm water
- Decoration for the eyes, buttons, etc. (for example, chocolate sprinkles, sugared violets, raisins)

1 Ask your child to put the butter or margarine, sugar, and corn syrup into a pan. You then melt them over a low heat and allow the mixture to cool.

2 Ask your child to sift the flour, baking powder, and spices into a bowl. When the butter mixture is cool, add it to the flour. Then tell your child to add the milk, and show him how to stir everything together.

3 Now show him how to do the final binding together using your hands to make a firm dough. Cover with plastic wrap and chill for 30 minutes.

4 Preheat the oven to 325°F (160°C). Place the dough onto a floured surface and show your child how to roll it out to ¼ in (5 mm) thickness. Show him how to cut out the gingerbread figures using the cookie cutters. Put the figures onto a greased baking sheet.

5 Put the baking sheet into the oven, and bake for 10 to 15 minutes, until the cookies are firm. Transfer to a wire rack to cool.

6 When completely cool, ask your child to sift the confectioners' sugar into a bowl and then add water to make frosting. Use it to stick on the decorations.

Worksheet 1

Learning height and length

Cut out each rod along the dotted lines.

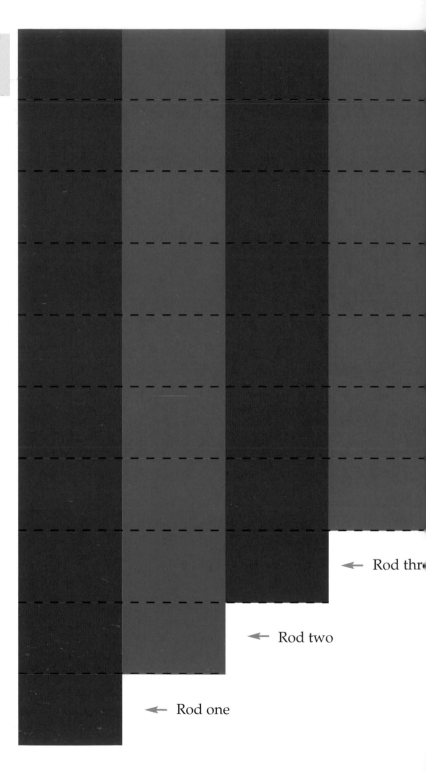

← Rod thr[e]

← Rod two

← Rod one

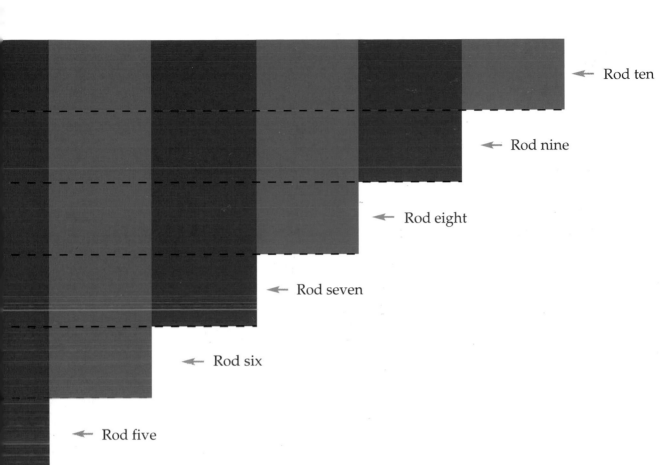

← Rod ten

← Rod nine

← Rod eight

← Rod seven

← Rod six

← Rod five

od four

Worksheet 2

Two-dimensional shapes

Matching circles

Matching squares

Matching triangles

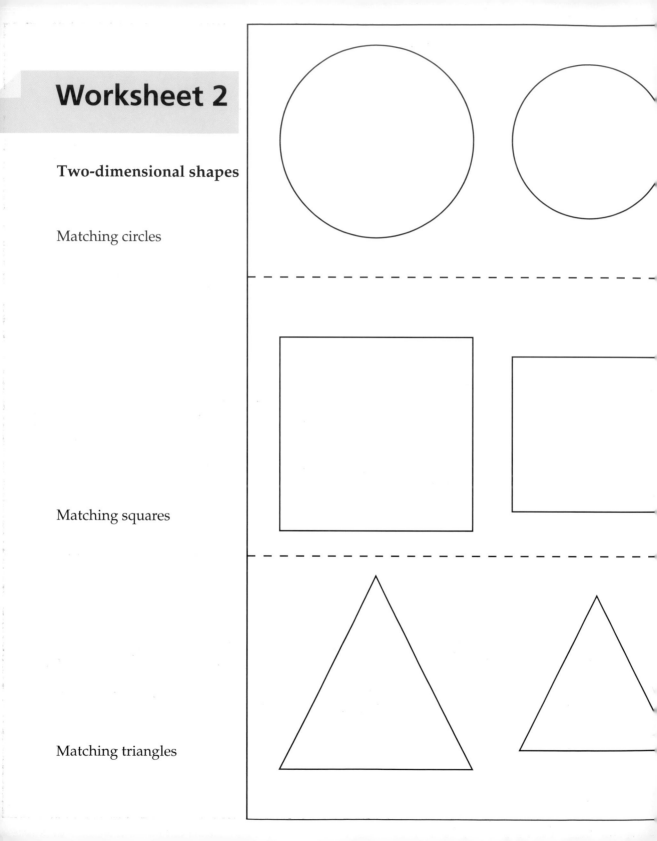

Circles

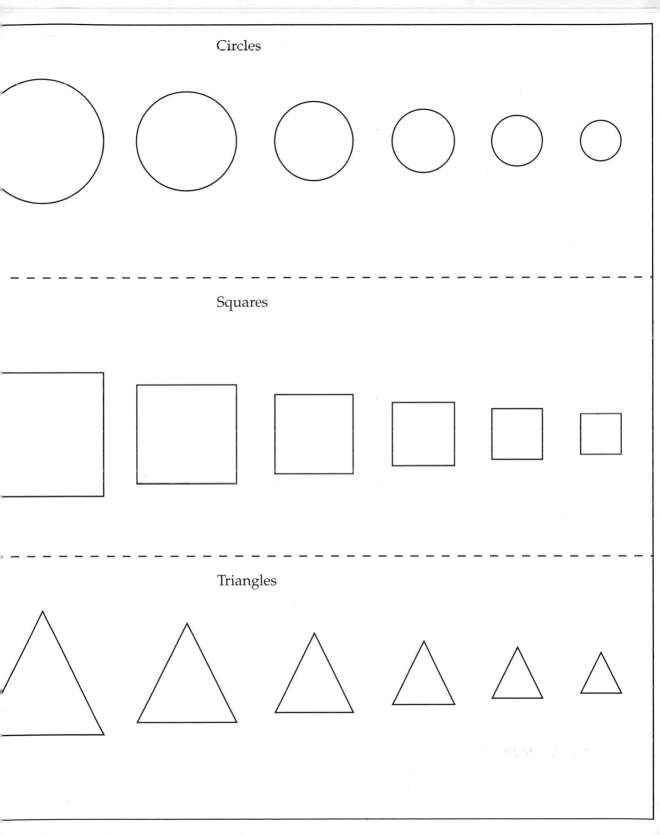

Squares

Triangles

Worksheet 3

The phonetic alphabet

Letters of the alphabet with
their phonetic sounds.

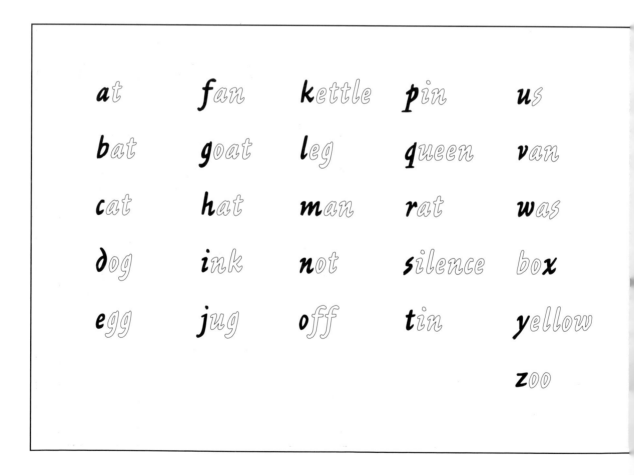

at	fan	kettle	pin	us
bat	goat	leg	queen	van
cat	hat	man	rat	was
dog	ink	not	silence	box
egg	jug	off	tin	yellow
				zoo

Worksheet 4

Identifying letters

Cut out each letter along the dotted lines.

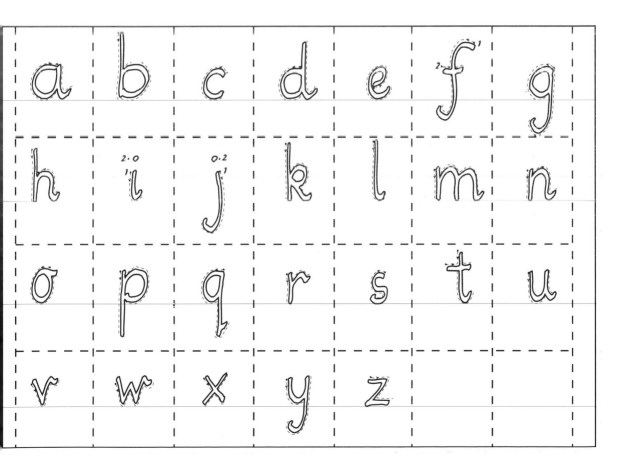

Worksheet 5

Word building

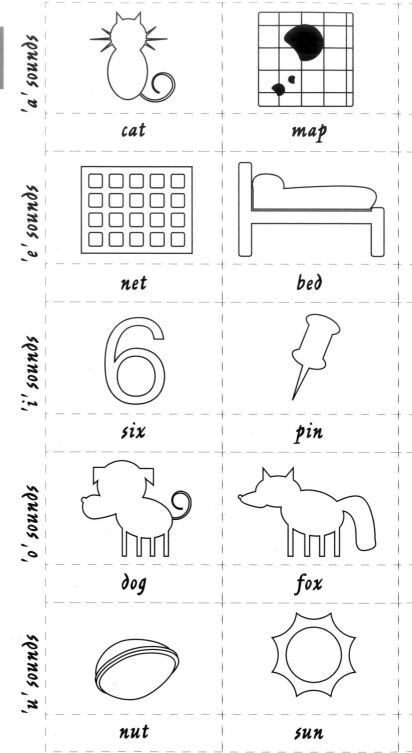

'a' sounds

cat   map

'e' sounds

net   bed

'i' sounds

six   pin

'o' sounds

dog   fox

'u' sounds

nut   sun

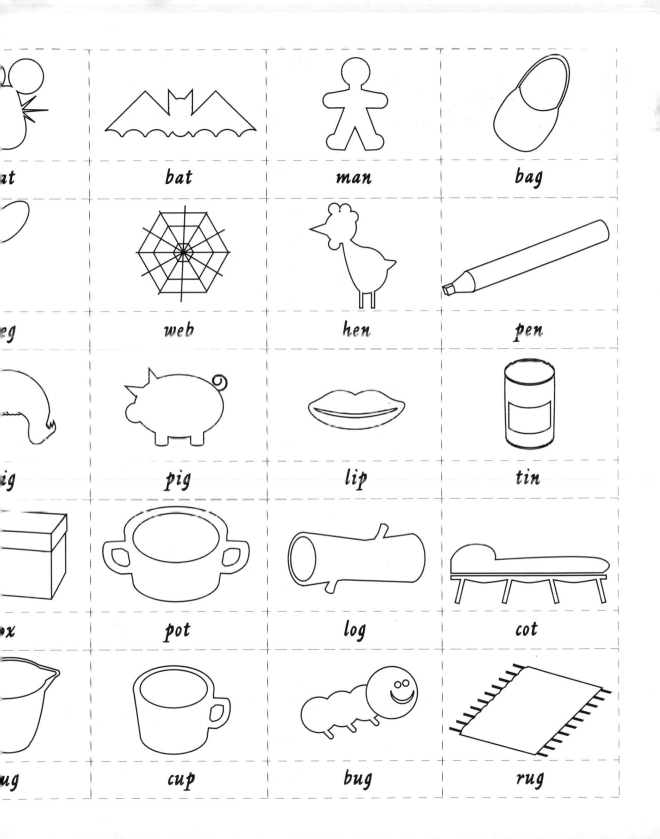

at	bat	man	bag
eg	web	hen	pen
ig	pig	lip	tin
ox	pot	log	cot
ug	cup	bug	rug

Worksheet 6

Constructing phrases

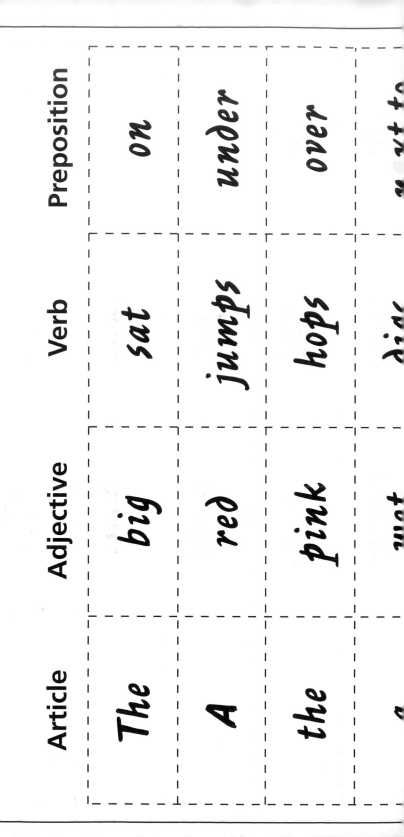

Article	Adjective	Verb	Preposition
The	big	sat	on
A	red	jumps	under
the	pink	hops	over

by		little
up		hot
runs		slim
put		thin
looks		soft
saw		spotted
goes		stripy
creeps		
rolls		

by

up

runs

put

looks

saw

goes

creeps

rolls

little

hot

slim

thin

soft

spotted

stripy

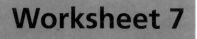

Worksheet 7

Make a flower puzzle

Petal	Roots	Stem	Leaves

Ovary	Stamen	Stigmas